FEARLESS WRITING

ESSAY GUIDE

STEP-BY-STEP INSTRUCTION FOR MIDDLE-SCHOOL WRITING

Written by Danielle Denega

Spark Publishing
A Division of Barnes & Noble
120 Fifth Avenue
New York, NY 10011
www.sparknotes.com

ISBN-13: 978-1-4114-9751-1
ISBN-10: 1-4114-9751-1

For more information, please visit *www.flashkidsbooks.com*
Please submit changes or report errors to *www.flashkidsbooks.com/errors*

Printed and bound in China

1 3 5 7 9 10 8 6 4 2

NOW THAT YOU'RE IN MIDDLE SCHOOL, ARE YOU WORRIED about the difficult writing projects your teachers are assigning? Does the thought of sitting down to write an essay or paper fill you with dread? Don't be fearful—BE FEARLESS! This Fearless Writing book will help guide you through the ins and outs of preparing for, writing, and revising your very own essay. Are you excited? You should be!

Writing is different from most other school subjects. In fact, some would say that writing is MORE FUN than most anything! Unlike math or science, writing does not require you to memorize formulas or equations. There are no clear-cut right and wrong answers here. What you will find, however, is a chance to express your thoughts and opinions through writing. Believe it or not, writing can be a good time!

The more you write, the better writer you will become, so practice, practice, practice! By writing in your free time, you will become more skilled, and those school assignments won't seem so bad after all. Check out the *Fearless Writing: Essay Workbook* for extra practice with essay writing. Here are some ideas to help you practice writing on your own:

Keep a journal in which you record your thoughts daily.
Write letters to friends and family members.
Write your very own autobiography—the story of your life.

You hold between your hands the key to your new life as a fearless writer. Your days of dreading those writing assignments are over.

LET'S BEGIN!

TABLE OF CONTENTS

CHAPTER 1

HOW TO WRITE ANY ESSAY

An essay is nothing more than a fairly short piece of writing that discusses the author's thoughts on a certain topic. There are many different types of essays: descriptive, cause-and-effect, narrative, and persuasive are just a few. Descriptive essays simply describe a person, place, thing, or idea. Cause-and-effect essays discuss the reasons for and results of things. Narrative essays tell the reader about a personal experience that the writer has had. Persuasive essays argue that the writer's opinion is correct. The later chapters of this book will discuss each of these types of essays in more detail.

Let's begin by taking a look at the basic steps to writing essays. These guidelines will work for almost any type of essay assignment you receive, so think of this as your go-to section for writing essays.

FIND OUT EXACTLY WHAT IS REQUIRED OF YOU

Okay, you've been assigned to write an essay. The very first thing you need to do is get all the facts. Before you start your essay, make sure you understand exactly what your teacher requires. Ask questions if you need to. It's much easier to get all the information from the start than waste any time or effort later. Use the following checklist to be sure you've covered all the bases:

- When is the essay due?
- Can I pick the essay topic myself or is there an assigned one? If I can choose my own essay topic, are there any restrictions on my choice?
- How many paragraphs should the essay be?
- Should the essay be done in a specific format, such as typed or double-spaced?
- Exactly what type of essay should I write?

ALLOW YOURSELF ENOUGH TIME TO WRITE YOUR ESSAY

One of the most important things to bear in mind when given any homework assignment is that you have to plan accordingly. This is especially true with essay writing. You'll need to leave yourself plenty of time to complete all the steps required to write a top-notch essay. There are five main stages to consider when planning how much time you'll need to complete your essay:

PREWRITING

This is the stage at which you organize your ideas. Decide upon a topic and do research, if necessary. Make an outline and/or graphic organizer of the thoughts, facts, and ideas to be included in your essay.

WRITING

This is the stage at which you create the first draft of your essay. Your first draft should include a thesis sentence, an introduction, a body, and a conclusion.

REVISING

This is the stage at which you should read your draft several times, and change its content and readability until you are completely satisfied.

EDITING AND PROOFREADING

This is the stage at which you should go back and fix any spelling, punctuation, and grammar mistakes in your essay.

PRESENTING

This is the stage at which you should make efforts to have your essay look as good as possible. Check the font and the font size and make sure it is consistent throughout your essay.

> **HOW MUCH TIME?**
>
> When it comes to writing, some people can do it quite quickly, and other people take a bit longer. Be realistic when scheduling time to do your essay. If you're a slower writer, you must accommodate for that. If you have a test the same day that your essay is due, or need to attend dance class or a soccer game on the days before, keep these things in mind! Don't overestimate how quickly you can complete the essay, especially if you are busy. Having a lot to do is no excuse for handing in anything less than your best.

CHOOSING YOUR OWN TOPIC

If your teacher is allowing you to choose the topic of your essay, you are one lucky student! Even if you don't particularly like writing, it's better to be able to pick your own homework assignment, isn't it?

Here are a few ways to choose a topic for your essay, or any other type of writing, for that matter:

BRAINSTORM

Never seen this word before? It's really just a fancy word that means "free thinking." To brainstorm, simply plop yourself down with a pen and paper and write down everything and anything that comes to mind. Even if your next thought is, *I can't write an essay about that*, just keep writing. The thoughts that immediately follow might be gems! The main goal is not to censor yourself. After you brainstorm, go back and examine the ideas you've jotted down. At least one of them will probably put you on the right track to an A-grade essay.

SURF THE WEB

The Internet is an endless source of information about, well . . . everything. If it exists, you can probably find out more about it on the web! A good way to start generating topic ideas is to go to general interest sites such as Yahoo.com or MSN.com. There you will find news stories and articles of the day. One of them might catch your eye.

SCAN THE LIBRARY OR BOOKSTORE SHELVES

An additional way to come up with an essay topic is to head to your local bookstore or library. Walk the aisles and scan the bookshelves. Check out the aisles you may not usually visit, like science fiction or history. This will inevitably spark ideas that will pop into your head.

REFER TO YOUR WRITER'S NOTEBOOK

A good place to seek out essay topic ideas is in a writer's notebook. A *what*? Don't worry; it's just a special name for a journal. It's a place where people write down things they think, see, hear, or read. Some people record their dreams, some people write down jokes they hear, and others just jot down random thoughts or experiences.

For example, here are a few things you may write in a writer's notebook as you sit in the park one day:

> This park is really pretty and peaceful. I wish there was a park like this closer to where I live. There should be more parks in general.

If you already have a writer's notebook, use it to *help* you brainstorm. Flip through its pages, scanning the things you've already written. More than likely, there are some nuggets that could make a great essay topic.

EXAMINE YOUR LIFE

Many essay assignments will ask that you write about yourself in some way. If that's the case, go back and examine your life to generate topic ideas. Go through photo albums, yearbooks, and memory boxes. They'll help jog your memory!

USING THE INTERNET TO RESEARCH A TOPIC

You have the luxury of being a student at a time when an endless source of information is available at the click of a mouse! The World Wide Web can be very valuable when researching your essay topic. But be warned that all Internet sites are not created equal, and some aren't even factual! Just about anyone can post information on the web. That means the information on there is not all well researched or even true. Play it safe, and stick to well-known, scholarly sites to be sure the information you are obtaining is accurate. A parent, teacher, or librarian can help you determine which sites are trustworthy.

TIPS FOR PICKING A TOPIC

- **Pick a cool topic:** You should aim to pick a topic that is interesting to you. Picking one that you find unappealing will only make completing your essay more difficult.

- **Be sure the information is out there:** If you will need to do research about the topic, be sure that sources are readily available.

- **Make it snappy!:** Time is of the essence, so choose a topic quickly! Your essay is actually going to be due at some point, so get down to it already. The more time you spend picking your topic, the less time you'll have to actually write the essay.

- **Remember the goal or purpose of the essay:** Make sure that you clearly understand the purpose of the essay that you've been assigned. This will greatly affect the topic you choose! For example, if you need to write a persuasive essay, pick a topic about which you are passionate. Or, if you have to write a narrative essay, opt for a topic about which you have personal experience.

AN ASSIGNED ESSAY TOPIC ISN'T ALWAYS A BAD THING

If your teacher has assigned the topic of your essay, there's not a whole lot you can do about it, so don't fight it. Of course, it seems much easier to write an essay on a topic you like, but having an assigned topic isn't the end of the world. Look at it as a chance to write about something you wouldn't normally pick yourself. Keep an open mind!

NARROWING DOWN THE POSSIBILITIES

You may find that many of the possible essay topics you've considered are simply too much to handle in one short essay. You'll need to narrow down your idea to make it more manageable. One technique for narrowing a topic is to make a topic web. Start with one idea and write it in the center of a blank page. Then, make spokes coming out from it, like on a bike. Write down any other thoughts related to that first topic on the spokes. Then, think about the spokes themselves and write down more new ideas that come to mind. Here is an example of a topic web:

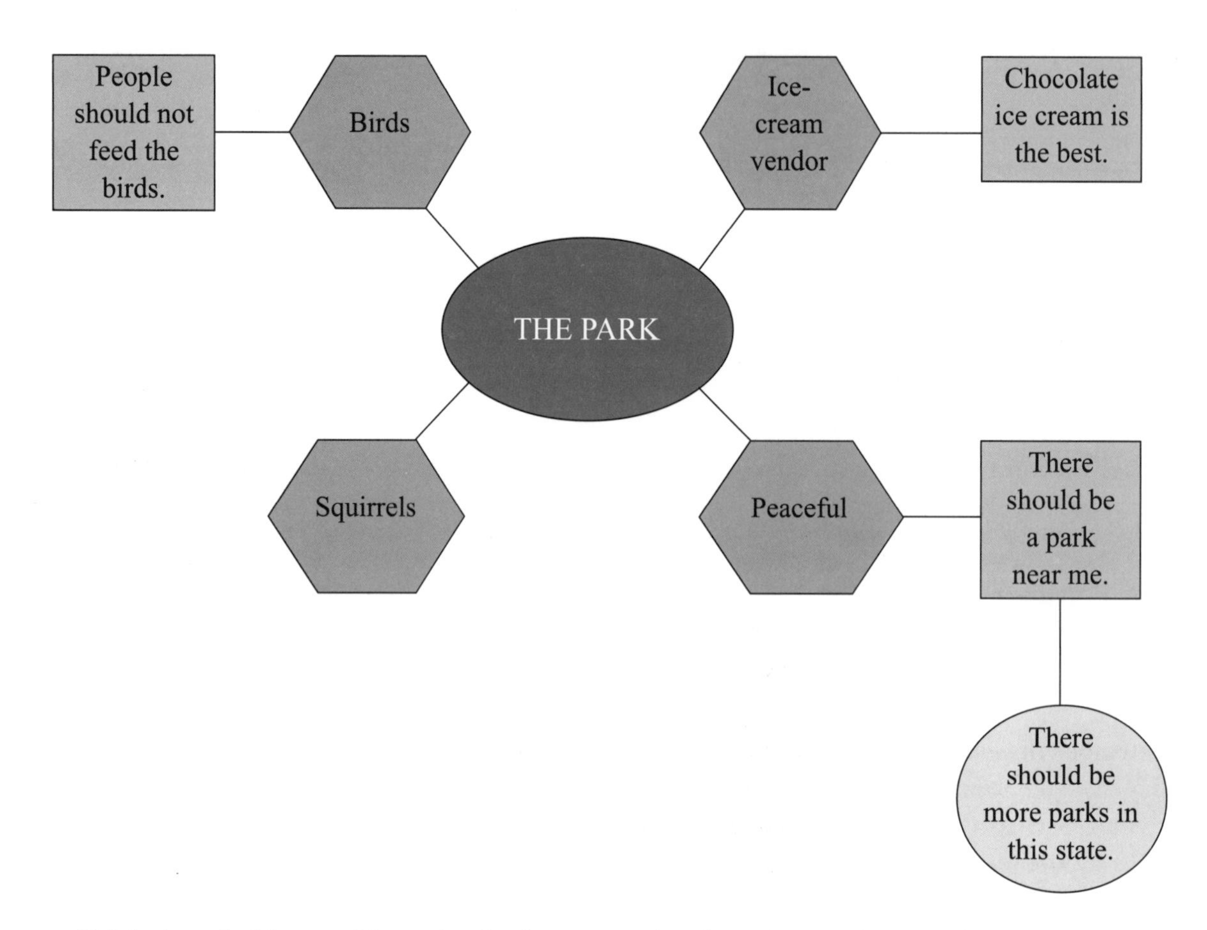

Think about it this way: If you simply choose to write about the park in general, you could write about hundreds of different things! This would make your essay seem unfocused. Rather than just writing about the park in general, follow the spokes of your topic web outward and pick a topic that is less overwhelming, such as the idea that there should be more parks in your state.

ORGANIZE YOUR IDEAS

There are many different tools you can use to help pinpoint the focus of your essay. Each of these graphic organizers below can be utilized when your teacher gives you a topic for an assignment and you need some help getting started. Once you've established the topic of your essay, you will undoubtedly have many ideas about it—probably too many to actually include in your essay! You'll need to rein in your thoughts on the topic, so try using any of the graphic organizers below to help. Keep in mind that each of these is best used for a specific type of essay, so pay attention to the specifics of each.

OPINION CHART

An opinion chart is a chart in which you write down your opinions or beliefs regarding a persuasive essay topic. Start by writing your opinion at the top of a blank page. Then, make a chart with four columns and four rows. In the first column, write down each of the main reasons for your opinion. In each column to the right of that reason, write a supporting detail.

Opinion: ________________			
Main Reasons for My Opinion	**Supporting Detail #1**	**Supporting Detail #2**	**Supporting Detail #3**

W'S CHART

This type of chart is helpful for narrative essays in which you need to hone in on the five W's: *who, what, where, when,* and *why.* Make a column for all of the five W's, and below each write down the information that answers the question.

Who?
What?
Where?
When?
Why?

SENSES CHART

This type of organizer can be helpful when writing a descriptive or narrative essay. There are five human senses: hearing, sight, smell, touch, and taste. Make a column for each sense, and below each write down what that sense experienced in relation to the topic.

Hearing	Sight	Smell	Touch	Taste

PLOT DIAGRAM

This type of graphic organizer can be useful when writing a narrative essay because it helps you sort out the action, plot, or story. The first diagram shows how a story should be organized. You can use the second diagram's blank spaces to write the exposition, rising action, climax, falling action, and resolution of your story.

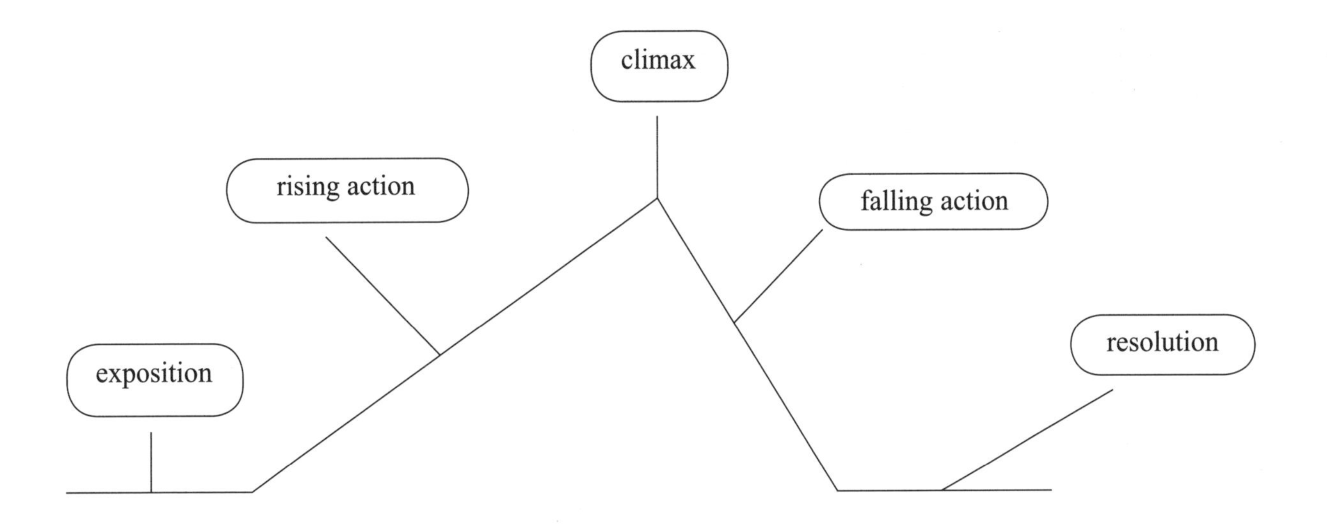

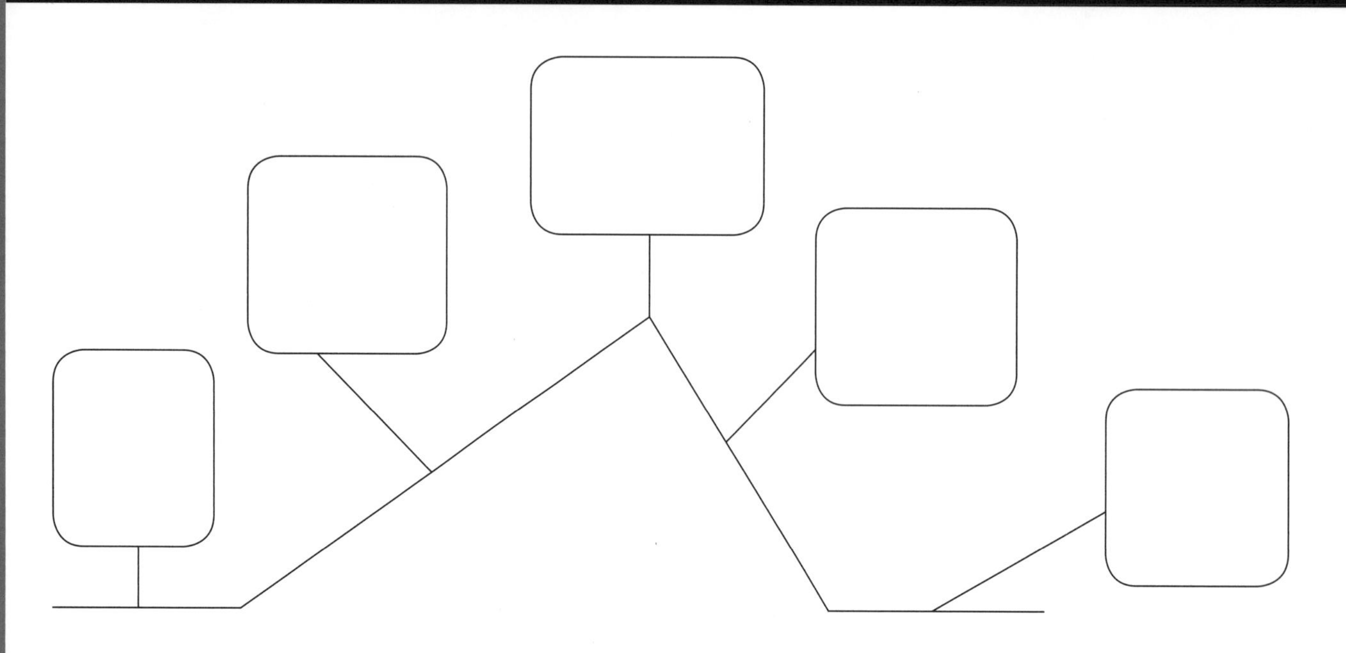

WRITING AN OUTLINE

Many teachers will require you to create an outline for your essay before you actually begin writing it. Outlines are basically just well-organized lists of the most important points in a piece of writing. It may seem like an unnecessary extra step, but outlines are worth the effort, because they make the actual writing process a piece of cake!

Remember those connect-the-dot drawings you used to make when you were young? The dots led your hand around the page so the drawing was complete in no time. An outline does the same thing! You jot your ideas down in an orderly way. Then when it's time to write your first draft, all you have to do is connect the ideas to make the essay complete. (There will be more about writing the first draft later in this chapter.)

Begin your outline by writing the thesis sentence of your essay at the top of the page. It will be part of your introduction paragraph. Here is an example of a thesis sentence:

Introduction
Thesis: The Kingston Space Museum is an awesome, interactive place to learn more about the science of space.

Next, write down at least three strong points that explain your main idea, leaving space below each to add a little bit of detail.

I. I learned about the planets.

  A.

  B.

II. I learned about the stars.

A.

B.

III. I saw a great space show.

A.

B.

Then, fill in a few supporting details below each of your main points.

I. I learned about the planets.

A. I saw an ecosphere that explores where life could exist in the universe and how it might look on Mars.

B. I saw and touched a 15-ton ancient meteorite.

II. I learned about the stars.

A. I found out what a supernova is.

B. I found information on how stars form and evolve.

III. I saw a great space show.

A. It showed how our Moon was created five billion years ago.

B. I felt what it might have been like when a meteorite hit Earth 65 million years ago.

Finally, add your conclusion paragraph.

Conclusion
Restate main idea: The Kingston Space Museum is a really cool place to learn more about space.

DRAFTS ARE JUST A STARTING POINT

So you have a topic for your essay assignment. You have organized your thoughts and ideas with a graphic organizer, and laid them out for yourself in an outline. Now you're ready to write your first draft. A draft, by definition, is not perfect. It's important to remember that. No piece of writing is faultless right out of the gate. Do you think the final versions of the Harry Potter books are exactly the way J.K. Rowling wrote them the first time? No way! Don't try to make a perfect first draft. Just put the words on the page without stopping after each phrase or sentence to evaluate it. You'll get to that later.

TIPS FOR WRITING A FIRST DRAFT

Ask yourself the following questions. You know you are good to go if you can answer "yes" to all of them before beginning your first draft:

- Have I established a clear, focused, manageable topic?
- Do I know enough or have I collected enough information about the topic to write a successful essay?
- Do I have strong supporting details with which to flesh out my essay?
- Have I organized all the information to be included in my essay?

THE PARTS OF AN ESSAY

Most likely your teacher will assign you to write a five-paragraph essay. That means exactly what it sounds like—your essay should have five paragraphs! Essays can be much longer than that, but starting out with a clearly defined format, like the five-paragraph essay, will teach you the basics before you try to tackle a longer essay. Let's take a look at each part of an essay.

THE INTRODUCTION

The first paragraph of any essay is called the introduction. The introductory paragraph is the place in which the writer establishes the topic and point of the essay. Whenever you meet someone new, you want to make a positive impression, right? Well, that's the goal of your introduction paragraph, too!

Your introduction should grab the reader's attention. To do this, you'll need to create a strong thesis sentence. A thesis sentence is a single statement that conveys the main idea of the essay. Your thesis sentence will have two parts: It tells the reader what the essay is about; it also tells the reader whether the essay is meant to describe, narrate, show a cause-and-effect relationship, or persuade.

Your introductory paragraph should also provide your reader with some background information about the topic of the essay. Don't assume that your reader knows about the subject matter already. Include a sentence or two to put the essay in context.

Here's a sample introduction to an essay about the space museum:

The Kingston Space Museum is an awesome, interactive place to learn more about the science of space.	thesis statement
The Space Museum is located on Main Street and has the largest planetarium in the country. Space museums mainly deal with the science of astronomy.	background
In the Kingston Space Museum I learned about planets, stars, and even got to see a space show!	details

THE BODY

The body paragraphs of an essay are the paragraphs that sit between the introduction and the conclusion—it's the middle! The body makes up the bulk of the piece of writing. For a five-paragraph essay, the body should consist of three paragraphs. These paragraphs are known as supporting paragraphs. That's because each body paragraph should be focused on a different reason that *supports* your main idea.

Develop one main supporting reason per body paragraph. The paragraph should discuss the reason and how it relates back to the main idea of the essay. These are called supporting details.

Let's take a look at the body paragraphs for an essay about the Space Museum:

The first reason that I think the Kingston Space Museum is awesome is because I learned more about the planets.	first supporting reason
I saw an ecosphere, or self-sustaining habitat, that explores where life could exist in the universe and how it might look on Mars. The ecosphere is contained in 39 inches of closed glass. I also saw a 15-ton ancient meteorite. It's a piece of ancient cosmic debris!	supporting details
The second reason that I enjoyed the Kingston Space Museum is because I learned more about stars.	second supporting reason
I found out that a supernova is a star that explodes and glows very brightly in the process. There is also a satellite dish and computer interactive that gives you information on how stars form and evolve.	supporting details
The third reason that I feel the Kingston Space Museum is fantastic is because I saw a great space show at the planetarium there.	third supporting reason
It showed how our Moon was created five billion years ago. It even simulated what it might have felt like when a meteorite hit Earth 65 million years ago.	supporting details

THE CONCLUSION

The fifth and final paragraph of a five-paragraph essay is called the conclusion paragraph. The conclusion should restate the main idea of the essay.

It's crucial that the conclusion be used to end your essay in an original and powerful manner. Give it some zing! The conclusion is your last shot at telling the reader that the information you've presented is important and valid. It is often also helpful if your conclusion contains a call to action, a suggestion for the reader, or offers the reader a thought or additional piece of information that will keep him or her thinking about the topic long after he or she puts down your essay.

Here is a sample conclusion paragraph for an essay on the space museum:

The Kingston Space Museum is a really cool place to learn more about space. It has great displays and interactive elements that taught me a lot about the planets and stars. I even got to see an amazing space show! I think that the Kingston Space Museum would be the perfect place to visit with your family or school.	restate the main idea suggestion for the reader

PUT IT ALL TOGETHER

Now, let's take a look at the full essay in draft form:

INTRODUCTION	The Kingston Space Museum is an awesome, interactive place to learn more about the science of space. The Space Museum is located on Main Street and has the largest planetarium in the country. Space museums mainly deal with the science of astronomy. In the Kingston Space Museum I learned about planets, stars, and even got to see a space show!	thesis statement background details
BODY	The first reason that I think the Kingston Space Museum is awesome is because I learned more about the planets. I saw an ecosphere, or self-sustaining habitat, that explores where life could exist in the universe and how it might look on Mars. The ecosphere is contained in 39 inches of closed glass. I also saw a 15-ton ancient meteorite. It's a piece of ancient cosmic debris!	first supporting reason supporting details
BODY	The second reason that I enjoyed the Kingston Space Museum is because I learned more about stars. I found out that a supernova is a star that explodes and glows very brightly in the process. There is also a satellite dish and computer interactive that gives you information on how stars form and evolve.	second supporting reason supporting details
BODY	The third reason that I feel the Kingston Space Museum is fantastic is because I saw a great space show at the planetarium there. It showed how our Moon was created five billion years ago. It even simulated what it might have felt like when a meteorite hit Earth 65 million years ago.	third supporting reason supporting details

C O N C L U S I O N	The Kingston Space Museum is a really cool place to learn more about space. It has great displays and interactive elements that taught me a lot about the planets and stars. I even got to see an amazing space show! I think that the Kingston Space Museum would be the perfect place to visit with your family or school.	restate the main idea/thesis suggestion for the reader

REVISING YOUR ESSAY

Guess what? If you've completed all the steps up to now, you have yourself a full draft of your essay. Nice work! But sadly, the work doesn't stop there. The hardest part is still yet to come. Revision is the hardest step in writing, but it's also the most important. No piece of writing is a polished gem right from the start. Most writing looks more like a muddy rock after the first draft is complete. The revision stage is the author's opportunity to polish that rock into a shiny diamond. If you're thinking, *I don't know how to do that*, have no fear! Just keep reading. If you use the following guidelines and tips to get you on your way, it'll be a pain-free experience.

THINGS TO KEEP IN MIND WHEN REVISING YOUR ESSAY

- **You've earned a rest.** After finishing your first draft, put your essay away for a while. Don't think about it, don't look at it, and don't talk about it. So far revising is a cinch, huh? You do have to go back to your essay eventually, but give yourself some down time. This is key to making the revision process successful. When you put a piece of writing down for a while and then return to it, you often have new perspectives on what you've put on the page. Writers call this having a "fresh eye." When you've been toiling over a draft for a while, you can lose sight of what parts of the essay are working and what is not. By giving yourself a time-out, you'll be able to see these problems more clearly than you would if you began revising immediately after finishing your draft.

- **You need to read your essay.** Aloud, that is! Reading your essay aloud to yourself and others is a great way to approach the revision process. Even if you are only reading the words for your own ears, actually hearing them aloud will often help you notice problems in the prose. If you read your essay to others, it's even more likely that you'll notice issues that need to be fixed as you revise. Other people will see your writing with an even fresher eye than you can. Their advice can be valuable, so pay attention!

- **You have to fulfill the purpose of the essay.** Each type of essay has a specific purpose. It might be to describe, persuade, and so on. Whatever the goal of the essay is, your essay needs to actually meet it! If you are describing something, will your readers feel like they've gone through the experience themselves? If you have written to persuade, will your essay convince your readers? These are the types of questions to ask yourself when revising your essay. For more detail on each specific type of essay, check out the later chapters of this book.

REVISING THE CONTENT OF YOUR ESSAY

Revising your writing for style and facts means making decisions about how you want to improve it. Look at your writing from a different point of view and identify areas that could be clearer, more interesting, more informative, or more convincing.

HAVE ENOUGH INFORMATION

A truly successful essay should be packed with facts, reasons, descriptions, etc. You can tell the reader something, but without solid support, your essay will fall flat on its face. If you don't already know tons about your topic, you'll need to do research. That might mean surfing the web, heading to the library, performing interviews, making personal observations, or anything else that will better inform you about your subject matter. Here's a sample sentence that doesn't have much support behind it:

> The Kingston Space Museum is a great place.

Okay, but *why* is it great? Here's a better one:

> The Kingston Space Museum is a great place to learn more about science because of its fun, interactive shows and displays.

Now the reader knows that the museum is a great place to learn, and that its displays are both fun and interactive.

BE CERTAIN YOUR INFORMATION IS IN A LOGICAL ORDER

As the author of your essay, you are responsible for guiding your reader through it. The reader is probably new to the topic (or at least new to your thoughts on the topic), so make it easy for the reader to navigate. Think of yourself as a wilderness guide. You've got the compass and know the destination, and it's your job to get everyone else there. Do this by placing the information in a logical order, such as chronological, order of significance, order of importance, or order of location. Use the approach that you think makes the most sense.

USE FOCUSED, CLEAR SENTENCES

All of your sentences should serve to support the main idea of your essay. Keep them on target! If a sentence seems like it's going off on a tangent, it probably is. Basically, all the pieces should come together to make one whole. Here's an example of a sentence that leads the reader away from the main idea instead of toward it:

> The Kingston Space Museum is near the History Museum, which is also an educational place to visit because they have huge dinosaur skeletons there.

While the History Museum might also be very interesting, it's not the focus of the essay. The essay is about the Space Museum, and *only* the Space Museum. Got it?

USE SMOOTH SENTENCES

Every sentence in your essay should go down like a glass of milk: nice and smooth. Sentences should not go down like an ear of corn on the cob: in short, choppy, messy bites. If you find that you have many short sentences in your essay, consider joining them into longer ones. This often makes for a smoother reading experience because the reader isn't pausing so frequently. Here is an example of sentences that are NOT smooth:

The Space Museum has planet displays. It has a meteorite display. The museum has a space show, too.

Here is a better, smoother sentence:

The Space Museum has displays about planets and meteorites, as well as a space show.

USE STRONG LANGUAGE

Using nouns, adjectives, verbs, and adverbs with some punch is a pretty easy way to kick up the energy of your essay. A noun is a person, place, or thing. Rather than using generic nouns, use very *specific* ones in your essay. For example, this sentence needs a little extra something to make it compelling to a reader:

The museum has exhibits.

Revised with stronger nouns, this sentence is now more interesting:

The Kingston Space Museum has star, Earth, and Moon exhibits.

A verb is the word in a sentence that shows action. Rather than using flat verbs, replace them with more vivid ones. In your first draft, you may have written:

During the space show, my seat and the floor moved.

Revised with vivid verbs in place, the same sentence could read:

During the space show, my seat shook and bounced and the floor vibrated.

Adjectives are words that describe nouns. They explain how something smells, tastes, sounds, looks, or feels. This sentence without adjectives falls flat:

The space show displayed all of the planets and stars in the Milky Way.

Adding adjectives makes the sentence read better:

The space show displayed all of the enormous planets and sparkling stars in the Milky Way.

Adverbs help describe verbs. They can tell the reader when, where, or how the action of the sentence took place. A sentence without adverbs might read:

I walked though the space museum observing the displays.

The revised sentence with adverbs inserted would look like:

I walked slowly though the space museum carefully observing the displays.

ADD AN INTERESTING TITLE

Topping off your essay with a relevant, intriguing title is a great way to reel in your reader before he or she has even read a word. It's often easier to wait until your essay is revised and in its final form before adding a title. That way, your title will reflect the essay more accurately.

MAKE YOUR OPENING AND CLOSING ZINGERS

The introduction and conclusion of your essay should each clearly state the main idea of the essay. The introduction should invite readers into the essay immediately, so that they'll keep reading. The conclusion should leave readers feeling satisfied that they've learned something about the topic, and even leave them wanting more! If your essay doesn't begin and end with gusto, consider revising.

OMIT EXTRA DETAILS

If you have collected tons of information about your topic, you may be tempted to pack it all in the essay simply because it's available to you. This is not a good way to approach your essay. Include only details that are relevant to the main idea of the essay. If you include too much extra information, your reader will lose sight of the essay's purpose.

USE A STRONG, PERSONAL VOICE

To make your essay stand out, you should write it in your own voice. Say what you truly think and feel about the topic to give it a genuine feeling. Even though your essay is most likely for a school assignment, it doesn't have to be overly formal or stuffy (unless, of course, your teacher has specified that it should be!). Write the way you speak. Just be sure to leave out slang terms. It's also crucial to make the voice of your essay enthusiastic and passionate. These feelings are contagious! If your essay expresses them, your reader will feel them, too.

NEVER PLAGIARIZE

Plagiarism is when one person takes the words of another and passes them off as his or her own without giving credit to the source. When writing essays, it might be tempting to do this because it seems like less work for you. But this is not a wise decision! Not only is plagiarism cheating, it's also illegal. Yes, *illegal*!

To avoid accidentally plagiarizing, do not copy information from your sources word for word. Copy down only the important parts of any statement, and when you use them in your essay, put them in your own words. Your voice is the one your teacher must be reading on the page, not the voice of the author of your source.

PROOFREADING YOUR ESSAY

Proofreading is another part of the revision process. It involves reading over your work very carefully in order to find errors in grammar, spelling, and format. The chapter at the end of this book will give you the lowdown on how to fix and avoid making common mistakes. It also contains a chart of proofreading marks, so you can mark up your essay like a professional editor! So flip to page 75 for more information. For quick reference, use the following checklist to be certain you looked for common mistakes:

____ My sentences all begin with a capital letter.
____ I used proper punctuation.
____ I spell-checked my essay on my computer and with my own eyes.
____ I indented each new paragraph.
____ I used all the parts of speech appropriately.

PRESENTING YOUR ESSAY

Wouldn't it be nice to live in a world in which appearances don't matter? Unfortunately, that's not reality. Your essay will be judged partly based on the way it looks, so make the effort to make it neat and presentable.

REWRITE OR REPRINT

Once you have completely revised your essay and fixed any errors, you'll need to make a fresh copy. That means either rewriting it neatly by hand, or printing out a clean copy of the revised document. Stick to blue or black ink if you are writing it by hand, and black ink if you are using a computer. If you handwrite your final draft and make an error, you could rewrite the entire essay or consider using correction fluid. Whatever you do, don't leave messy cross-outs on the page!

USE CLEAN, WHITE PAPER

Use only clean, bright white paper for the final copy of your essay. Save the colored or patterned paper for personal notes and letters.

KEEP IT CLEAN

By the time your essay makes it to your teacher's hand, it will have traveled pretty far: from your house, to your backpack, to your locker, and then finally to class with you. Make sure that it stays clean in its travels! Placing your essay in a folder will protect it from crumpling. Be sure it doesn't have any run-ins with food, beverages, science experiments, or pets. Your teacher won't appreciate seeing your breakfast on your essay!

ENHANCE IT WITH ART AND A COVER

Your teacher may not require that you include a cover for your essay, but it can't hurt, right? A cover will make your essay look even more appealing and professional. Artwork can also help enhance your essay. Adding photos or drawings to the back of your essay will show that you really took an interest in the topic. Spending a few extra minutes to add these things will show your teacher that you want your essay to stand out.

CHAPTER 2

DESCRIPTIVE ESSAYS

Put simply, a descriptive essay *describes* something, usually a person, place, or thing. It can also describe a memory or experience. *Describe* means to represent or give an account of something in words.

The purpose of a descriptive essay is to involve the reader enough so that he or she can actually visualize the things being described. You want to show, not tell. Therefore, it is important to use specific and concrete language. In order to describe something, you have to provide the reader with all sorts of details about how something appears, tastes, smells, feels, or sounds. Details like these are called sensory details, and they're very important to include in a descriptive essay. We'll go over this in more detail later in the chapter.

If you think about it, you describe things all the time when you talk to people. When a friend asks you about your spring-break vacation, you don't just say that it was "fine" or "okay," do you? More than likely, you tell your friend about your vacation by describing it. You may say that you went to the Caribbean and that the water was turquoise and warm, like bathwater. You might also say that the sand was powdery, soft, and white. You could also mention that you went swimming with dolphins at a special center. The dolphins were huge and felt rubbery, and you fed them stinky, dead fish. Based on all of these details, your friend now has a pretty good idea what your vacation destination was like, huh?

But what does this have to do with your descriptive essay assignment? Writing a descriptive essay is just like describing something to a friend. It should not scare you! You describe things all the time in your everyday life, so putting it down on paper is no big deal. Let's check it out . . .

ALLOW YOURSELF ENOUGH TIME TO WRITE YOUR DESCRIPTIVE ESSAY

There are the five basic steps required to write an excellent descriptive essay. Think carefully about how long it will take you to perform each of these steps, and be honest with yourself. Also keep in mind that if you are like most young adults, school isn't the only thing going on in your life. You've got sports, volunteer work, dance class, tutoring, and clubs to think about, too! Consider how much time these things take up when scheduling time for your descriptive essay assignment. Make sure you have enough time to complete all of these five steps:

PREWRITING

Prewriting includes all the steps that lead up to your first draft. This is the stage at which you decide what it is you want to describe, if that's been left up to you. Then, you should begin organizing your thoughts by using a graphic organizer, such as the five senses chart on page 11. Then, further plan out your description by making an outline.

WRITING

Now is the time to put your thoughts into complete sentences. Your first draft should include an introduction, a body, and a conclusion. Descriptive essays should also strive to use special writing techniques, like those discussed on page 30, and many details.

REVISING

This is the stage at which you should reread your draft several times. Shift around words, sentences, even paragraphs, until you are happy with the way it reads. Descriptive essays should create a vivid mental image for the reader, and the revision stage is a good time to make sure that's the case.

EDITING AND PROOFREADING

Go back and fix any spelling, punctuation, and grammar mistakes in your descriptive essay.

PRESENTING

Make your essay look neat and presentable. A great addition to descriptive essays is artwork. You've just painted a picture with words, now paint one for real! Add it to the end of the essay or use it as a cover. Head back to page 21 in the first chapter of this book for even more information about presentation.

THE TOPIC OF YOUR DESCRIPTIVE ESSAY

You now understand your mission, and whether or not you like it, you have to accept this mission (or risk getting a failing grade!). Step one of your essay mission is picking what to write about. (If your teacher assigned a topic to you, feel free to skip right to the next section.) You might already have ideas swirling around in your head, but if not, there are many helpful tips to help you choose the topic of your essay.

BRAINSTORM

A great way to think of topics for your essay is to brainstorm. Brainstorming is a way to encourage the thoughts and ideas to come out of your brain. Simply sit down with a pen and paper and think—that's right; just sit there and THINK. Ponder the things about your essay assignment that you find intriguing. Write them down as they pop into your head. Don't censor yourself, either! Just write down anything and everything you think of.

REFER TO YOUR WRITER'S NOTEBOOK

A lot of people keep journals or diaries in which they write down thoughts, feelings, and observations. A writer's notebook serves the same purpose, but with a goal in mind: giving you things to write about! If you already have a journal or writer's notebook, pick it up and read old entries. There may be a descriptive essay topic hiding in there!

THINK OF PEOPLE, PLACES, AND THINGS

When was the last time you really stopped to think long and hard about something as simple as a person, place, or thing? Descriptive essays are primarily based on concrete details, therefore an ideal topic is something in your immediate world, such as a person you know, a place you've visited, or a thing you're familiar with. You might consider writing about a grandparent, Yankee Stadium, or your favorite blanket from childhood.

OTHER THINGS TO KEEP IN MIND WHEN PICKING A TOPIC

When picking a topic for your descriptive essay, it's helpful to pick a topic with which you have experience. The goal of a descriptive essay is to show the reader your topic by painting a mental picture. If you have actually experienced or perceived something yourself, it's got potential as a topic. Let's say you love baseball and want to describe the game in which the Red Sox won the World Series. If you weren't actually there, or did not at least watch it on television, describing the game to someone else is going to be tricky, isn't it? All the details necessary to write a solid description won't come out of thin air! The bottom line is that if you've actually observed or experienced it, it's fair game as a topic.

"SHOW, DON'T TELL" YOUR READER

Before you choose a topic, remember one thing: You'll need to include details, details, details. Rather than just *telling* your reader, *show* the reader by including all the juicy details that you can recollect. These details help your reader feel as though they were there, too!

ORGANIZE YOUR IDEAS

Once you've decided upon a topic, you need to organize your thoughts before you begin writing. It may seem like an extra step, but it'll actually save you time in the long run and make for a better essay.

TRY A FIVE SENSES CHART

A graphic organizer can be a helpful tool when writing a descriptive essay. A five senses chart is a great way to include sensory details in your essay. You begin by making a column for each of the five senses: hearing, sight, touch, taste, and smell. Then in each column write down what that sense experienced in relation to the topic.

Here's an example of a five senses chart for a baseball game:

Hearing	Sight	Smell	Touch	Taste
vendors yelling	thousands of people	hot dogs and cotton candy	hard plastic seat	hot dog with mustard and sauerkraut
crowd cheering	green field and brown diamond	fresh-cut grass	cold soda in my hand	sweet soda
announcer saying who's at bat	my dad next to me	my dad's cologne	cool air	
bat cracking when it hits the ball	players in uniforms		fuzzy sweater	

WRITE AN OUTLINE

Your teacher may ask you to hand in a topic outline for your descriptive essay. Even if it's not required of you, an outline is a really helpful tool to get your essay going. Outlines enable you to gather all the thoughts and details in your head and put them in a logical order—one that will make sense to your reader.

Follow the example below, and begin by writing down your thesis sentence under the Introduction part of the outline. A thesis sentence is the place in which you tell your reader what your essay is about and what its goal is. In the case of descriptive essays, the goal is, well . . . to describe something!

Introduction
Thesis: Throughout my life, the willow tree has come to mean a great deal to me.

Then, write down three main points, leaving space below each to add a little bit of supporting detail.

I. Tire Swing
   A. Held the tire swing I played on as a child
   B. Swing was fun and scary at the same time

II. Hide-and-Seek

A. Climbed up it to hide

B. Scraped my legs

III. Hammock

A. Held the hammock I laid on as a teenager

B. Dark, quiet place to read and nap

C. Let me disappear from the world for a while

Then add the conclusion portion of the outline. Restate the main idea and then add a sentence or two that will leave the reader feeling satisfied.

Conclusion
Restate main idea: The willow tree was a place where I could play, hide, and escape.
Additional thought: The tree is now gone and I miss it dearly.

You're done! Okay, that's not quite true, but you have taken a huge step toward *really* being done with your descriptive essay assignment. Pat yourself on the back!

WRITING THE FIRST DRAFT OF YOUR DESCRIPTIVE ESSAY

Use your outline as a guide to writing the first draft of your essay. The main points are already down on paper, so the current task is simply to flesh them out. Bear in mind that you are writing the *draft* of your essay. A draft, by definition, is not final. The best way to approach a first draft is just to write. It's actually as easy as it sounds! Just put the words on the page. Don't stop to critique each sentence as you write it. You'll have a chance to change things later.

THE PARTS OF A DESCRIPTIVE ESSAY

Let's break down the components of an essay so that you know what to do when it comes time to draft yours. All essays have three main parts: an introduction, a body, and a conclusion. In a descriptive essay, each of these parts should act to further illustrate your main idea. Your reader did not observe the person, place, or thing you are describing. Nor did your reader live through the experience or have the feeling. So use every word to your advantage in order to create a strong image in the mind of your reader.

In the introduction of a descriptive essay, you should state your main idea in a clear thesis sentence. This sentence tells the reader what the topic and point of your essay is, so make it a good one! Keep in mind that your reader may not know much about the topic, so your introduction should also give a small amount of background info. Here is an example of an introduction for a descriptive essay about skiing:

I started skiing when I was four years old, and at first I didn't enjoy it. I fell a lot and the cold snow would creep into my boots and the sleeves of my jacket. I'd get scared of soaring above the ground on the chairlift. But as I've gotten older, skiing is a sport that I have come to love for several reasons: being outdoors, the adrenaline rush of hurling down a mountain, and competitive racing.

Next, the body of your descriptive essay should have at least three paragraphs. Each body paragraph should be focused on a different reason that supports your main idea. Let's take a look at a sample body paragraph about skiing:

I love to ski so much now because I adore being in the outdoors. The air around me at the top of a mountain is clean, crisp, and refreshing. When it snows, the flakes swirl around me as I ski and creep up my nostrils, freezing the end of my nose. Trees line the trails and their branches are weighed down with freshly fallen snow. Standing on the peak of a mountain is like being closer to the moon and stars; I feel more connected to them because I feel so far away from the rest of the world when I'm up that high. There is a rush of cold air against the exposed parts of my face, and all I hear are my own skis cutting softly into the snow as I ski quickly down the mountain.

Lastly, the conclusion of a descriptive essay should . . . well, conclude things! This is the paragraph where you restate the main idea of the essay as well as the supporting reasons you talked about in the body of the essay. The conclusion of your descriptive essay should also include a final thought or idea about the topic. It should be one that leaves the reader feeling satisfied or makes him or her keep thinking about your essay long after finishing reading it.

For an essay about skiing, a conclusion paragraph might look like the following:

There are many reasons that I've come to love skiing, but the three that stand out most to me are spending time outdoors, the thrill of speeding down the mountain, and racing. Skiing is a beautiful sport because of the serene environment around you. When that aspect is combined with the excitement of racing down a mountain, especially during a competition, it's an unbeatable feeling. I can't wait until summer is over so I can head back up into the powder-covered mountains again, and then beat someone to the bottom!

USING SENSORY DETAILS

The most important thing to remember about writing a descriptive essay is that you must illustrate the main idea for your reader, rather than simply telling what it is. The best way to do this is by using sensory details.

Sensory details describe what each of your five senses perceived. You'll need to tell the reader the things you saw, smelled, heard, tasted, and felt. Here is an example of a descriptive essay paragraph that uses sensory details:

smell
The scent of old fish and popcorn filled my nostrils as the ferry pulled

sight sound
away from the dock. The clouds above parted and the squeal of a

taste
small child echoed behind us. The saltiness in the air crept across my tongue,

feel
and I clutched the calloused, dry hand of my father very tightly.

You have a pretty good idea of what the ferry experience was like because of the many sensory details the author has shared. They help paint a vivid image for the reader!

INJECT YOUR DESCRIPTIVE ESSAY WITH EMOTION

It is also important to add details about how you feel or felt emotionally about the topic of your essay. Your feelings and emotions are unique to you, so by including them, you're adding your personal stamp to the essay. Think about which details you can include to ensure that your reader develops an emotional impression. For example, you could add the following sentences to enhance the paragraph above:

smell
The scent of old fish and popcorn filled my nostrils as the ferry pulled away

emotion
from the dock. I felt a sense of longing, as though I were leaving something

sight sound
significant in the past. The clouds above parted and the squeal of a small child

taste
echoed behind us. The saltiness in the air crept across my tongue, and I clutched

feel emotion
the calloused, dry hand of my father very tightly. I was instantly comforted.

By adding these additional feelings to the description, you've injected your essay with emotion, which makes it more powerful for the reader.

USE VIVID LANGUAGE

When writing a descriptive essay, be certain to use fresh and varied vocabulary. For example, in the paragraph above, the author says scents "filled my nostrils" rather than just saying, "I smelled." A child "squealed" rather than "yelled," and "I clutched" rather than "I held." Strong words like these make any description more exciting to read.

OTHER WRITING TECHNIQUES

Here are a few writing techniques that you should try to use to give your descriptive essay that little something extra:

- **Allusion:** a reference made to something common that the author assumes the reader will understand.
- **Simile:** a figure of speech that compares things using the words *like* or *as*.
- **Metaphor:** a figure of speech that compares things without using the words *like* or *as*.
- **Symbol:** a real thing that is used to represent something else.
- **Hyperbole:** an exaggeration to stress a point.
- **Oxymoron:** places two words that mean the opposite next to each other in a sentence.
- **Personification:** gives human qualities to things that are not human.

DESCRIPTIVE ESSAY REVISION CHECKLIST

You're almost done! Now that your draft is complete, you can take a break from it to get some perspective on how it could be made better. When you check back on it, refer to the list below. It contains things that should be considered when revising your descriptive essay. (For even more information about how to revise your writing, flip back to page 17 in the first chapter of this book.)

____ Does my introduction contain a strong thesis sentence?
____ Does my introduction give the reader some background information about the topic so the reader can put things in context?
____ Did I include at least three reasons that support the main idea, each reason in a new paragraph?
____ Did I add sensory details obtained through observation?
____ Have I included emotion and feelings in my description?

____ Have I used strong language to make my description more exciting?
____ Have I utilized writing techniques, such as metaphor and simile, to enhance my description?
____ Does my conclusion restate the main idea?
____ Does my conclusion leave the reader feeling satisfied and with a clear mental picture of my topic?
____ Have I checked my descriptive essay for grammar, punctuation, and spelling errors?

WRITING A DESCRIPTIVE ESSAY FOR A TEST

At some point in time, you will be given a test comprised of topics on which you have to write an essay on the spot. You've already read all about how to write descriptive essays, so you're one step ahead! Now, get clued in on a few more things that will take the fear out of essay tests:

DECIPHER THE QUESTION

Teachers and test writers like to use their own language on tests. Strange, but true. Many descriptive essay questions will be straightforward, simply asking you to describe something. But, if you see the words "discuss," "illustrate," or "develop," a descriptive essay could be in order, too.

BE AWARE OF TIME

Unlike homework essay assignments for which you can plan ahead and give a topic a lot of thought, essay tests mean that time is limited. So don't waste any!

USE YOUR HEAD

When writing a descriptive essay, you may often perform observations to better be able to describe your subject. But on a test, you more than likely won't be able to do this! Be ready to draw directly from your memory.

TAKE THE STEPS

Follow the steps for writing a descriptive essay that are outlined in this chapter. Just be quick about it! First and foremost, identify what the main idea of your essay will be. Write a brief outline, then draft your essay. Finally, reread your answer for content and grammar. Be sure to include writing techniques and lots and lots of details.

SAMPLE DESCRIPTIVE ESSAY

On the next page is a sample of a descriptive essay using the topic outlined earlier in this chapter. Pay special attention to the words on the right—they show the important elements that need to be included in a descriptive essay.

Behind my parents' house, in the winding woods of the Hudson River Valley, my father planted the sapling of a weeping willow tree. It was 1978—the year I was born. Throughout my life, the willow tree has come to mean a great deal to me.	background information about topic thesis sentence
When I was a diminutive, freckle-faced child, the willow seemed able to hold the weight of the world, or at least my weight. From its heftiest branch, my father hung a bright yellow rope attached to a tire to make a swing. I spent hours hanging upside down in the tire, with my dark, silky hair brushing the ground as I dangled. I'd let the blood rush to my head, making my round face pink, until I'd whip myself upright again. My older brother would push me and I'd wrap my legs around the swing, locking my ankles together. I'd laugh heartily because I was a little bit afraid and a little bit exhilarated at the same time.	vivid word choice sensory details emotion
After dark, on summer nights, the neighborhood kids played hide-and-seek in the glow of lightning bugs. When it was my turn to hide, I'd hoist my body up into the willow tree, scraping my legs on its rough, gray branches until I was out of sight of the seeker. There I'd sit and wait, listening for the sounds of approaching footsteps or the cry of a player who'd been "found" to signal the end of the game.	vivid word choice sensory details
Eventually, my father replaced the worn tire swing with a beige, woven hammock. The hammock was suspended from the branches of the willow tree and was situated in its perpetual shadow. On the occasions when the world had become too much to handle, I'd duck into the shade of the willow tree and sit in the hammock. When I looked upward, the branches of the tree spread out over me, reaching toward the sky a little further every year. Sometimes when my parents were at work, I'd slip into the hammock with a book and eventually fall asleep. When my mother finally beckoned me inside, my thighs would be indented with the mesh pattern of the hammock.	sensory details emotion personification vivid word choice sensory details
Last year, a bolt of lightning hit the willow tree, setting it ablaze momentarily and shattering its trunk. Servicemen came to cut down the damaged, now threatening, tree, and I watched safely from a distance. The hum of chain saws and the cracking of wood made me wince. When its trunk finally rested in pieces on the ground, it was as though I'd been cut to pieces, too. The willow tree had become a place to play, hide, and escape. I knew I would miss it dearly.	vivid word choice sensory details emotion

CHAPTER 3

CAUSE-AND-EFFECT ESSAYS

Perhaps you've been assigned a cause-and-effect essay. You're not even sure what that means, let alone how to write one for this assignment. But you can do this—promise! Break it down by word: *cause* means a reason for an action or condition; an *effect* is a result—it's something that inevitably follows a cause. So a cause-and-effect essay discusses why things happen (causes) and what happens as a result (effects).

Still feeling hesitant? Don't! Think about causes and effects in terms of your everyday life. Suppose you got a D on your last history test. As a result, your parents took away your video-game console, grounded you for the weekend, and have gotten you a tutor. The *cause* in this situation is the bad grade on the test. The *effects* are the loss of the video games, the grounding, and the tutor. One cause can have many effects.

Cause-and-effect situations can work in the opposite direction, too. Sometimes multiple causes can create one effect. For example, you enjoy playing soccer, you want to do something cool with your summer, and you love visiting upstate New York. These are three causes that have one effect: You go to soccer camp for the summer in upstate New York.

See? This stuff happens to you all the time—you just don't think about it in these terms. For a cause-and-effect essay, you just have to translate this line of thinking into essay form. Let's get started!

ALLOW YOURSELF ENOUGH TIME TO WRITE YOUR CAUSE-AND-EFFECT ESSAY

Writing a cause-and-effect essay requires a series of five steps that can't be avoided if you want to lock in a good grade. Allow yourself plenty of time to complete the assignment, especially if you have other obligations in your life. If you have baseball practice or need to do volunteer work the same week that your essay is due, or if you have other papers or tests on its due date, you need to schedule time for these things! Being busy is not an excuse for turning in an essay that isn't your best effort. So don't even think about skipping any one of the following:

PREWRITING

This is all the stuff that needs to happen before you can actually start to write your cause-and-effect essay. You'll need to pick a topic, if one hasn't been assigned to you. Your cause-and-effect essay may need to include facts, details, statistics, and quotes from experts. That means you'll have to do research. (Turn to Chapter 6 for more information on doing research.) Once that's accomplished, create a cause-and-effect graphic organizer, like the one on page 37. Then, move on to an outline, which is detailed on page 39 of this chapter.

WRITING

Use your cause-and-effect graphic organizer and outline to help you put your thoughts into complete sentences. Your first draft should include an introduction, a body, and a conclusion. Aim to include transition words and supporting details throughout your draft.

REVISING

This is the stage at which you should read your cause-and-effect essay repeatedly, and change it until it meets its goal: demonstrating the cause-effect relationship.

EDITING AND PROOFREADING

This is the stage at which you should go back and fix any spelling, punctuation, and grammar mistakes in your cause-and-effect essay.

PRESENTING

Your cause-and-effect essay should be neat and clean. It can also include art, graphs, or charts that further illustrate the cause-effect relationship you present in the essay. For example, for an essay that includes information about New York City being multiracial, you might include a pie chart showing the breakdown of ethnicities in that city.

THE TOPIC OF YOUR CAUSE-AND-EFFECT ESSAY

If your teacher has assigned the topic of your essay, you can move right along to the next section of this chapter. But if the topic is up to you, all eyes here! When the subject of an assignment has been left completely open ended, it can seem intimidating. Cause-and-effect essays can be about just about anything, as long as there is a clear cause-effect relationship in the topic. They can be about you or your beliefs, science, history, public policies . . . there really is no cap on the possibilities. Here are a few suggestions to help you get started:

BRAINSTORM

A great way to begin thinking of topics for your cause-and-effect essay is to brainstorm. To brainstorm, all you have to do is think freely. Sit down with a notebook and pen and think, "cause and effect." Whatever comes to mind, write it down. Keep writing ideas until you've filled the page (or until you feel tapped out). Then go back and review all those little thoughts and nuggets. One of them is bound to work for your essay! If not, distract yourself with something else and try brainstorming again.

SURF THE WEB

Another way to think of ideas for an essay is to read general interest sites on the Internet (Yahoo.com and MSN.com, for example). Sites such as these offer news stories and articles that change daily. One of them could very well make a perfect cause-and-effect topic.

SCAN THE LIBRARY OR BOOKSTORE SHELVES

Just strolling the aisles of your neighborhood bookstore or local library is another way to develop topic ideas. Read titles, scour tables, and pick up anything that looks or sounds appealing. Seeing what others have written about may spark an idea in your own head.

REFER TO YOUR WRITER'S NOTEBOOK

A writer's notebook is not all that different from a journal or diary. It's just a notebook in which you write down thoughts. This notebook then acts as a bank of topics. When you have a writing assignment, you can flip through the pages of your writer's notebook to recall ideas you've already had. If you don't already have a writer's notebook, start one now. This certainly won't be the last essay you'll ever have to write!

OTHER THINGS TO KEEP IN MIND WHEN PICKING A TOPIC

Cause-and-effect essays should serve one of two purposes: They should either persuade the reader into believing something, or simply inform the reader of something. Regardless of which route you choose, you'll have to include facts, details, and statistics to prove the cause-and-effect relationship. So make sure there's enough information available about your topic.

If you pick a topic that is personal to you, you'll probably have all the facts and reasons you need already in your head. It's your life, after all! But, if you go with a topic that's about something you're not too familiar with, you'll have to do some research to find facts and statistics with which to support the cause-effect relationship.

BE CERTAIN THE CAUSE-EFFECT RELATIONSHIP IS CLEAR

The most important part of a cause-and-effect essay is to actually demonstrate a clear relationship between the cause and its effects or vice versa. When trying to pick a topic for your essay, make sure that it's very obvious that the actions and their results are directly related. For example:

Effect: I was late for school today.
Cause 1: The bus arrived early, so I missed it.
Cause 2: My mom had to give me a ride, but the car wouldn't start.
Cause 3: I woke up late.

All three of the causes are very clearly related to the effect: being late. Each one contributed to the end result. Here's an example of an indirect relationship:

Effect: I was late for school today.
Cause 1: My homework wasn't done.
Cause 2: We ran out of cereal.
Cause 3: My backpack is ripped.

These three causes are not directly responsible for the end result. They may have happened on the same day and contributed to a bad morning, but that's about it.

ORGANIZE YOUR IDEAS

It is especially important when starting a cause-and-effect essay to organize your thoughts before writing. You will most likely be dealing with research material and the facts and figures that support your topic. This information needs to be mapped out before you begin writing in order to present your ideas clearly. Here are a couple of ways to get organized before you put pen to paper.

MAKE A CAUSE-AND-EFFECT CHART

Graphic organizers are simply drawings, or graphics, that offer you a place to start sorting out your thoughts. If you are writing an essay in which you will talk about multiple effects and their single cause, your graphic organizer should look like this:

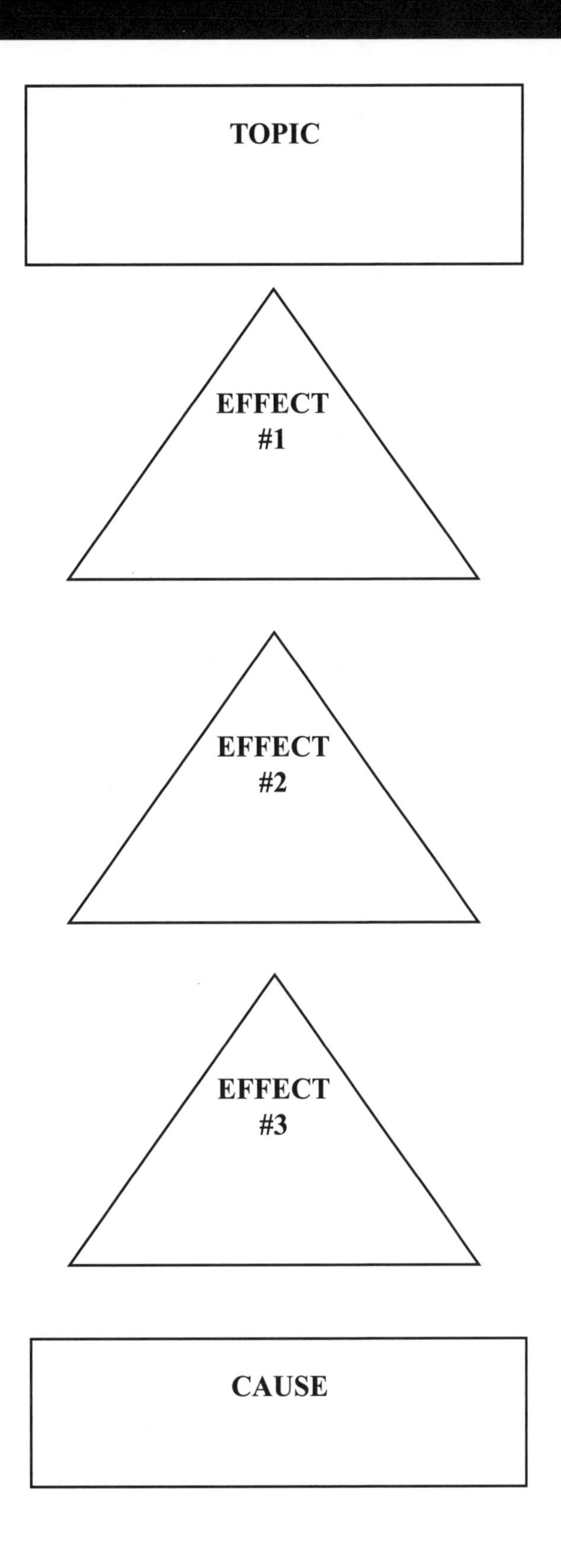
TOPIC
EFFECT
#1
EFFECT
#2
EFFECT
#3
CAUSE

If you've decided to write an essay in which you discuss several causes and the single effect of them, the graphic organizer should look like this:

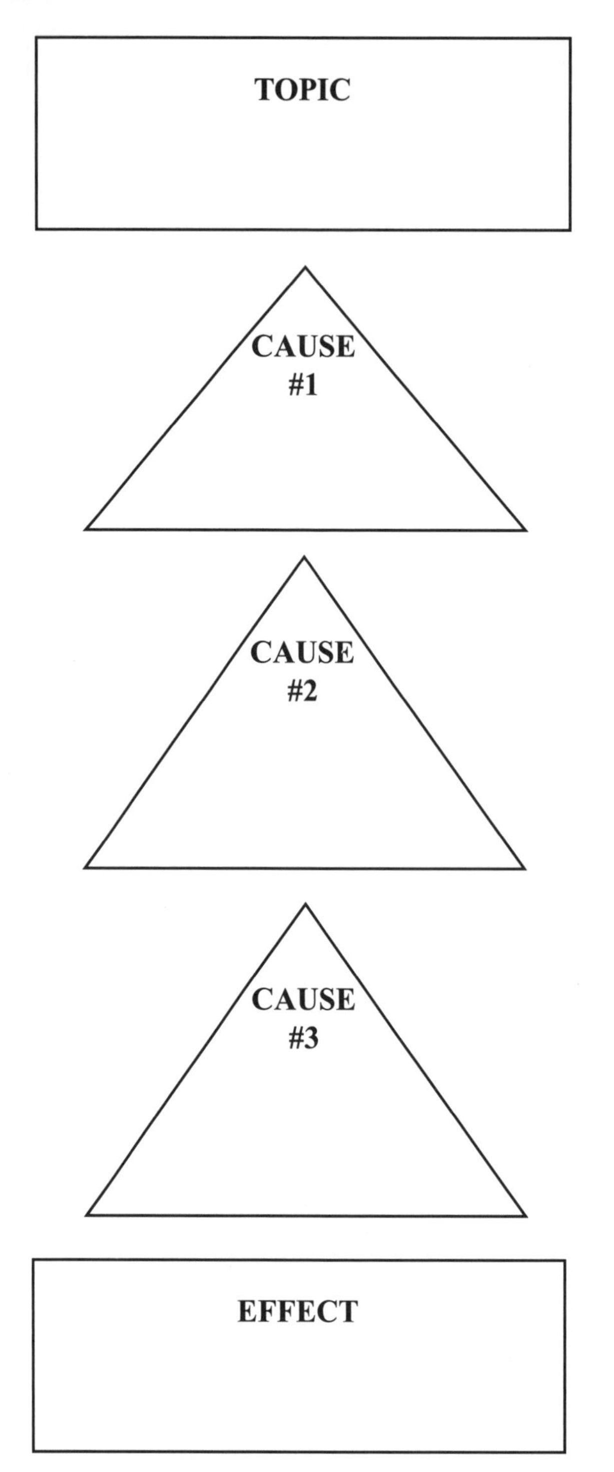

WRITE AN OUTLINE

The next step to a successful essay is an outline. Many teachers will actually ask you to hand in an outline. They'll review it to be sure you are going in the right direction with your essay. Once it is approved, you are then free to continue working. If your teacher does not require you to hand in an outline, it does not mean that you can skip this step! It is very important that you take the time to create an outline. Outlines allow you to further organize your thoughts and ideas and put them in an order that makes sense.

Start by writing your thesis sentence on the top of the page under the introduction portion of the outline. A thesis sentence tells the reader what the essay is about, and what its goal or purpose is.

Introduction
Thesis: My favorite city in the United States is New York, and there are several things that have caused me to feel this way: its racial diversity, its cultural activities, and its close proximity to places like the beach and mountains.

Then, write down at least three strong causes, leaving space below each to add a little bit of detail.

I. **Cause 1:** New York is racially diverse.

A. Ellis Island

B. 27 percent Hispanic, more than 28 percent African American, and almost 10 percent Asian

C. Melting pot

II. **Cause 2:** New York has lots of great cultural things to do.

A. Theater/Broadway shows

B. Ballet

C. Museums

D. Opera and other music

III. **Cause 3:** New York is close to the mountains and the beach.

A. Long Island and New Jersey beaches

B. Catskill mountains

Then add the conclusion portion of the outline. Restate the main idea of the essay:

Conclusion
Restate main idea: Because of its racial diversity, culture, and closeness to the beach and mountains, New York has become my favorite city in the country.

You should be feeling pretty good about yourself right now because you've just completed a large portion of the work involved in writing your cause-and-effect essay. Now, it's time to start writing, and your outline will make that part of the process go much more quickly and smoothly.

WRITING THE FIRST DRAFT OF YOUR CAUSE-AND-EFFECT ESSAY

Your first draft should be a free-for-all of words. Do not stop to think about spelling, punctuation, or even style. You will have the opportunity to worry about all of that during the revision stage of the game.

THE PARTS OF A CAUSE-AND-EFFECT ESSAY

All essays have three main components: an introduction, a body, and a conclusion. Cause-and-effect essays are no different!

In the introduction of a cause-and-effect essay, you should state the cause-and-effect relationship of your topic in a concise thesis sentence. A thesis sentence is one well thought-out sentence that serves two purposes: It tells the reader what the essay is about, and it tells the reader what the purpose of the essay is. What the essay is about is up to you or your teacher, but in every cause-and-effect essay, the thesis sentence should explain that the purpose of the essay is to prove or illustrate a cause-and-effect relationship. The introduction of a cause-and-effect essay should also include some extra background info about your topic to help the reader understand it a little better. For example, if you were writing a cause-and-effect essay about some of the drawbacks of modern-day inventions, your introduction paragraph might include something like this:

> Great inventions have the power to better our lives. But, inventions also have the ability to damage us. Television is an example of a modern-day invention that has had negative effects on society, including increasing obesity, lowering sensitivity to violence, and causing eyestrain.

The body of your cause-and-effect essay should then cover each of your causes or effects, depending on how you've decided to present the topic. Each new body paragraph should be focused on a different cause that supports a single effect, or on a different effect that supports a single cause. The body should also include additional details, facts, and/or statistics that further illustrate the focus of each paragraph.

Put the body paragraphs in an order that makes the most sense for the topic. This could be most important to least important or vice versa; most obvious to least obvious or vice versa; or even chronologically, if that works best.

> The most significant effect of the invention of television is that it has contributed to the obesity problem in America. Television consumption leads to hours spent inactive. The mindless nature of television also increases mindless snacking. The United States is one of the fattest countries in the world, and Americans watch more television than almost anyone in the world. The correlation is hard to ignore.

To write a successful conclusion paragraph for your cause-and-effect essay, you must restate the main idea. The conclusion should leave the reader with a feeling that you've proven your point. It should also strive to have the reader thinking about your essay long after reading it. For example:

Television has the potential to be a powerful tool. It allows us to share and spread information very quickly and easily to masses of people. But, unfortunately, the advent of television into mainstream America has also had many negative effects on our culture, such as contributing to obesity, causing eye strain, and making us less sensitive to violence. It's time Americans stopped ignoring these problems and reconsider what they choose to view and how often they watch television.

SUPPORTING THE CAUSE-AND-EFFECT RELATIONSHIP

Your cause-and-effect essay may be about something personal to you, in which case, most of the information you will need to include in your essay is already in your head. But, many cause-and-effect essay topics will require that you supply the reader with additional facts and details. This means you'll have to do some research!

LOOK IT UP

The Internet is a fantastic source of information about every topic you can imagine. If you don't have access to it at home, use computers at your school or local library. Be careful of using sites that aren't trustworthy, however. Just because someone posted it on the web doesn't make it true. For help choosing sites that are worthwhile, ask a parent or librarian. Here's an example of a bit of information you might find on the Internet that you could include in your essay:

Manatees are among the North American animals on the endangered species list.

OFFER STATISTICS

A good way to help support the cause-and-effect relationship you're describing is to cite statistics related to your point. For example:

Bamboo consists of about 99 percent of a panda's diet.

INCLUDE YOUR OWN OBSERVATIONS

Another good way to demonstrate the cause-and-effect relationship in your essay is to give your reader first-hand observations. If you don't know enough about something to write about it, go see it for yourself!

There are more small children playing in Oakfield Park than there are playing in Emmet Street Park on weekdays.

ASK THE EXPERTS

Experts in the subject about which you are writing can be very helpful to your essay. They can offer solid facts and information to help support your main idea, and you can quote them directly. Direct quotations make your essay seem very official and professional! For example:

> According to Civil Engineer Erik McHale, "The new, widened roadways in town should help the traffic problem considerably."

USE TRANSITION WORDS

Transition words are words or phrases that connect one thought to another within a sentence or paragraph. In cause-and-effect writing, it is especially important to utilize transition words. Transition words help solidify the direct relationship you are showing between your causes and their effect, or between your effects and their cause. For example:

> My car won't start. It has no gas left in the tank.

These thoughts could be independent of one another. Is the lack of gas responsible for the car not starting? It's not 100 percent clear to the reader. But if the sentence includes a transitional phrase, it becomes clear:

> My car won't start due to the fact that it has no gas left in the tank.

Now the reader can clearly see the cause-and-effect relationship in the thought. The cause is that there is no gas, and its effect is that the car will not start. See how much more sense that makes?

TRANSITION WORDS

Here is a list of other transition words that you should incorporate into your cause-and-effect essay:

Because	If . . . then
Consequently	Thus
As a result of	Due to
Therefore	Have caused

CAUSE-AND-EFFECT ESSAY REVISION CHECKLIST

It's time to evaluate your initial effort. For the full blow-by-blow on how to revise the content, flow, and language of your writing, head back to the first chapter of this book. If you've already been there and done that, just use the following checklist to make sure you covered all the major points:

____ Does my introduction contain a thesis sentence that makes the cause-effect relationship obvious?
____ Does my introduction give the reader background information about the topic I discuss in the rest of the essay?
____ Did I include at least three very strong points that support the main idea, with each point in a new paragraph?
____ Did I back up the points in my cause-and-effect essay with details, facts, expert opinions, observations, and/or statistics?
____ Have I used transition terms and phrases?
____ Does my conclusion restate the cause(s) and effect(s)?
____ Does my conclusion end the essay in a thoughtful way that leaves the reader feeling satisfied?
____ Have I checked my cause-and-effect essay for grammar, punctuation, and spelling errors?

WRITING A CAUSE-AND-EFFECT ESSAY FOR A TEST

Chances are that at some point in your career as a student, you will need to write a cause-and-effect essay in a test situation. Again, have no fear! The following are some tips and guidelines to get you through it with ease.

DECIPHER THE QUESTION

Read the test question slowly and carefully to be sure you understand its meaning. Essay questions often seem as though they're written in some sort of secret teacher code. But the code can be broken! If a test question asks you to write an essay in any of the following ways, it's really asking that you write a cause-and-effect essay:

"What are the causes of X?"
"What led to X?"
"Why did X occur?"
"Why does X happen?"
"What would be the effects of X?"

Terms such as "explain," "review," and "prove" can also signal that a cause-and-effect essay is the way to go.

BE AWARE OF TIME

Time is the biggest factor when writing a cause-and-effect essay for a test. Unlike a homework assignment, you are on the clock big time, so get going!

USE YOUR HEAD

In test situations you will probably not be able to research your cause-and-effect topic, so be prepared to pull information directly from the information bank in your head: your brain!

TAKE THE STEPS

Follow the steps for writing a cause-and-effect essay that are outlined in this chapter. Start by figuring out what the main idea of your answer will be. Then write a brief outline and draft your essay. Finally, reread your answer for content and grammar. When rereading your answer, be absolutely certain it demonstrates the cause-effect relationship. Also try to use transitional words to make your essay seem more polished and well written.

SAMPLE CAUSE-AND-EFFECT ESSAY

Here is a sample cause-and-effect essay that discusses the topic outlined earlier in this chapter.

I have traveled throughout the United States extensively because my father is in the Army. I have lived in many different cities. My favorite city in the United States is New York, and there are several things that have caused me to feel this way: its racial diversity, its cultural activities, and its close proximity to places like the beach and mountains. ← Thesis sentence

cause 1 → The first reason I adore New York is because it is so racially diverse. No matter what neighborhood you're in, the streets of New York are full of people whose ethnicity is so varied, it's hard to figure out what it is half the time! ← observations New York's Ellis Island has served as a portal for millions of people from different countries starting in the late 1800s. ← supporting details So many types of people poured into New York that it became known as a melting pot—a place where all cultures blend together. Now, nearly 27 percent claim Hispanic heritage, more than 28 percent are African American, and almost 10 percent are Asian. ← statistic

cause 2 → Another reason I think New York is the best city in the country is due to the fact that it has lots of great cultural things to do. ← transition word It offers world-renowned theater and musicals. It is also home to The New York City Ballet Company, which performs at the stunning Lincoln Center. New York City also houses many of the world's great museums, such as the Museum of Modern Art, the Guggenheim, and the American Museum of Natural History. ← supporting details Music venues are also widespread in New York, such as the Metropolitan Opera.

cause 3 → A third cause for my liking New York so much is that it is situated near both the mountains and the beach. When you live in a city, it's great to be able to leave it once in a while so that you may reconnect with nature. The pristine beaches of New Jersey are popular spots for New Yorkers to escape to because they are easily accessible by train. ← supporting details

The Hamptons, a celebrity stomping ground, is only a few hours away via bus. In addition, the picturesque Catskill Mountains are another nearby oasis for New Yorkers. The Catskills offer outdoor activities such as skiing and apple picking.

New York City is full of racial diversity and culture, and is ideal because it's close to the beach and mountains. These factors have caused New York to become my favorite city in the country. I can truly say, I love NY! ← restate main idea

CHAPTER 4

NARRATIVE ESSAYS

A *narrative* is just a story, so try to move past the fancy name. Most narratives are about you, and there's no subject you know better, right? Being assigned a narrative essay isn't anything to be stressed over! It can be about a person, event, or activity in your life. The other thing about narratives or personal stories is that they contain some sort of action. And the best stories aren't just enjoyable or amusing but have a point to make or an idea to pass on.

Writing a narrative essay is no big deal if you think about how often you do it without really thinking about it. When you go on vacation, do you come home and tell your friends all about it? When something interesting happens at school, do you go home and share it with your family? Any kind of story you might tell is a narrative. You do it all the time! In this chapter we'll help you hone your talent and learn to write narratives for school assignments. It'll teach you how to tell a more interesting story—inside and outside the classroom.

ALLOW YOURSELF ENOUGH TIME TO WRITE YOUR NARRATIVE ESSAY

Scheduling and managing your time well is very important, especially if you are as busy as most students your age. You'll need to give some thought to how much time you should set aside for your essay assignment. You may have sports practice, dance classes, piano lessons, babysitting jobs, and any number of other things going on around the time that your essay is due. Responsibilities such as these are great! They make you well-rounded and interesting. However, these responsibilities should not serve as excuses for not completing your essay.

There are the five steps to consider when planning how much time you'll need to complete your narrative essay. Skipping any of them will just make the next step harder, so it's best to accept the process for what it is.

PREWRITING

This is your chance to collect the information you need to start writing. Most important, pick your topic! Then use a graphic organizer, such as the plot diagram on page 11, to help define the parts of your story. Next, create an outline of the thoughts and ideas to be included in your essay.

WRITING

Use your plot diagram and outline to guide you as you write the first draft of your story. Your first draft should include an introduction, a body, and a conclusion. Aim to include many details, emotion, and vivid language in your narrative essay.

REVISING

This is the stage at which you should read your draft several times, and change it until you are completely satisfied. Your narrative essay should tell an interesting, detail-filled story that shares a common human experience.

EDITING AND PROOFREADING

Now, you should go back and fix any spelling, punctuation, and grammar mistakes in your essay.

PRESENTING

Finally, make efforts to have your essay look fantastic on the outside. A narrative essay is all about you, so add a personal touch, such as artwork or photographs (with permission!) to enhance the story you've shared.

THE TOPIC OF YOUR NARRATIVE ESSAY

If you're lucky, your teacher has opted to let you choose the topic of your narrative essay. If not, you can skip right to the next section! Picking a topic about which to write a story may seem overwhelming—there are so many things to choose from! Or it may seem like your brain is suddenly dried up like the Sahara. Nothing's coming to mind! If that's the case, keep reading for a few pointers on how to get the wheels in your head turning.

BRAINSTORM

Brainstorming is simply concentrated, uncensored thought. Anything that pops into your head is fair game. You never know what weird little nugget might develop into a full story, so write everything down, no matter what it is. Don't stop to think that an idea is silly or boring; just put it on the table.

REFER TO YOUR WRITER'S NOTEBOOK

A good place to search for ideas is in your writer's notebook. A writer's notebook is really just a special name for a journal or diary. It's a place to write down your thoughts and observations, experiences, and basically anything else that strikes you. If you've already got one, use it to your advantage. It is full of possible narrative essay ideas! If you don't already have a writer's notebook or other type of journal, start one now! Having a writer's notebook will definitely prove helpful no matter which type of essay you've been assigned to write.

MAKE A TIMELINE OF YOUR LIFE

When trying to think of stories about yourself or things in your life, it can be helpful to write a timeline of your life. Start by writing down your earliest memories, and just keep going, filling the timeline with additional memories and milestones. Timelines help jog your memory about all the fascinating things that have happened to you. One of those things will probably make a killer essay topic!

MAKE LIFE LISTS

Life lists are exactly what their name implies: lists you make about your life—things such as Best Moments of My Life, The Worst Things That Have Ever Happened to Me, The Funniest Things I've Ever Seen, The Saddest Day of My Life, My Favorite Places, or Favorite Things to Do. When you start recalling all of the things that have happened in your life in this manner, you'll find that narrative essay ideas will start springing off the page.

OTHER THINGS TO KEEP IN MIND WHEN PICKING A TOPIC

Vivid details make a story come to life. Whatever topic you choose for your narrative essay assignment, make it one that you can support with lots of details and feelings. This chapter will cover what details to include more thoroughly later. If you think of a potential topic, but can't remember all of the details clearly, it's not the best option. Stick with a topic that you recall very well.

THE TOPIC SHOULD REFLECT THE HUMAN EXPERIENCE

The human what?! The human experience is a fancy term for things that are universally experienced by almost all people in a similar way: Death makes us sad; newborn babies make us happy; feeling loved makes us feel safe; losing love makes us feel vulnerable. The occasion or person you decide to discuss in your narrative essay should allow the reader to reflect on the human experience. It should make the reader think, *I know exactly what the author means because that's happened to me!* or *I've felt that way too!*

WHERE SHOULD MY NARRATIVE ESSAY START?

Before you begin writing, you will need to decide on the order in which you'll present the plot. There are several ways to tell your narrative. The first way is chronologically. When you tell a story in chronological order, you tell it from beginning to end. This is the way it would happen in real time. You could also reverse that order and tell your story from end to beginning. Many writers find it exciting to begin a story in *medias res,* which means "in the middle of things." They start a story right smack in the middle, move to the end, and *then* explain the beginning.

ORGANIZE YOUR IDEAS

Before you begin writing, you must sit down and decide how to organize your narrative. There are many ways to present your story, and you may be overwhelmed when you sit down to write if you hadn't yet organized your thoughts and ideas. Here are some ideas to help you get organized.

GRAPHIC ORGANIZERS: MAKE A PLOT DIAGRAM

The main action or events that move a story along are called the plot. A plot has five parts: an exposition, a rising action, a climax, a falling action, and a resolution.

At the beginning of most stories there is an exposition. In the exposition, the characters are introduced. In the case of your personal narrative, you are one of the characters. So is anyone else who is involved or present. The exposition may also tell the reader where the story is set, which is the time and place.

Next, there is a rising action. This is the part of a story in which the conflict becomes clear, and the character(s) (that's you!) try to deal with it. The rising action should build suspense. Get the reader to the point at which he or she can't *wait* to see what happens next in the story.

Then, the conflict builds to a climax. The climax is the turning point or high point of the story. The climax contains the most excitement or drama because everything you have read thus far has been building up to it.

Next, there is a falling action, which is whatever happens after the climax. It's the point at which the author starts to lead the reader toward the end of the story. The drama becomes less intense in the falling action.

Finally, there is a resolution. The resolution is the part of the story in which the problems have worked themselves out, allowing the story to end.

The five parts of a plot can be best illustrated in a plot diagram. See page 11 to see how a plot diagram is made.

CREATE A STORY MAP

If your teacher has asked that you hand in an outline for your narrative essay, this next part will walk you through it. An outline for a story is actually called a story map, because it maps out the major points in an organized way. (Actually, even if your teacher has not asked for a story map, you should do one anyway, so keep reading!) Story maps may seem like a nuisance, but they really are helpful. They act as a loose shell, sketching out the basic premise of your narrative. Story maps are great because if you take the time and effort to make one, it'll be much easier when you write your first draft. A lot of the work will already have been done!

Start with an introduction/exposition. Write down what characters are involved in the story. Also include the setting, which is the time and place. Then, write a thesis sentence. Include the parts of a good story: rising actions, climax, falling actions, and a resolution. And finally, restate the main idea in your conclusion.

Here is a sample story map:

My Story Map

Exposition/Introduction

Characters: Me and Pedro Martinez

Setting: Seventh grade

Thesis sentence: I never expected to be friends with the "new kid," let alone learn anything from him.

Rising Actions:

1. Met Pedro in gym class and thought we were very different from one another.
2. Pedro didn't know how to play hockey, so he asked me to teach him.

3. I taught Pedro to play hockey and he turned out to be good!

Climax: Pedro thanked me for teaching him and offered to teach me something in return.

Falling Action: Pedro tutored me in Spanish and we started to really like one another.

Resolution: Pedro and I are now the closest of friends.

Restate thesis: Sometimes you find friendship in unexpected places, at unexpected times.

If you've made it this far, pat yourself on the back! Your story map is complete, which means a huge chunk of the work is done. Now, on to drafting your narrative essay . . .

WRITING THE FIRST DRAFT OF YOUR NARRATIVE ESSAY

When writing an essay, or any other piece of writing for that matter, always bear in mind that your first draft is nothing more than a place to start. It's important to simply write down whatever you want to say without stopping after each phrase or sentence to self-evaluate. You'll have a chance to do that later, when you revise your draft, so don't try to do both steps at the same time. It'll only leave you feeling frustrated. More on that later in this chapter . . .

THE PARTS OF A NARRATIVE ESSAY

Before you begin writing your draft, it's important that you have a strong grasp of each part of a standard narrative essay. All essays have three main parts: an introduction, a body, and a conclusion. Remember that you're telling a story, so each part of your essay should carry the story along in a way that will keep your reader interested.

The introduction of a narrative essay can act as the exposition of your story, if you like. It should include a thesis sentence that lets the reader know the topic of the essay, and what its ultimate goal or message is. Even though you're telling a story in your narrative essay, it should still have a point! And, recall from earlier in this chapter that the objective of a narrative essay is to discuss something having to do with the human experience, or a universal idea or feeling. Your reader should end your essay feeling as though you touched a chord because you reminded him or her of something common to all people. Here is an example of narrative writing that touches upon a topic everyone can relate to:

> Making a huge change, like moving to a new place, is one of the scariest but most rewarding things a person can do. Last year, my family and I moved 3,000 miles away from the home and school I knew so well. The experience could have scared me, but I didn't let it.

The body of your narrative essay should have as many paragraphs as it takes to tell the rest of the plot and all the important details of the story. Sometimes, when you are telling a story, it makes sense to have more paragraphs in order to get all the details in, or to keep the momentum of the story. If you feel like you need it, it's fine to make this type of essay a bit longer than one of the other types of essays.

Here's an example of a narrative essay body paragraph:

On the first day at my new school, I sat timidly at my desk during homeroom. The room buzzed as students chatted quietly to one another. I spoke to no one, and no one spoke to me. I stared at the huge, white clock on the wall, willing its hands to point to 3 PM. But then I remembered what my grandfather told me before we left: When you show a genuine interest in other people, they'll show an interest in you. I looked down at the laces of my brand-new sneakers, took a deep breath, and leaned over to the girl at the desk next to mine. I explained that it was my first day, and asked her how long she had been at this school and whether or not she liked it. Her round, freckled face lit up with a smile, and she answered me right away. By the end of our conversation, I had an invitation to sit with her at lunchtime!

The conclusion of a narrative should reflect on the meaning or importance of your story. That is, you should tie in the whole human experience idea again. Your conclusion should serve to further connect you and your reader by reminding the reader of the universal truth or feeling you touch on in your narrative. The plot should be completely wrapped up by the conclusion paragraph:

My new school reminded me that with big risk come big rewards. I embraced the change as an opportunity rather than a hurdle. Now I have great new friends, I made the basketball team, and best of all, I have more confidence in myself. I guess my grandfather was right after all!

FIRST-PERSON POINT OF VIEW

Most narrative essay assignments require that the story be about you. Your essay could be about a personal event from your past, an ongoing experience you're having, or an observation you made about something in the world. This means that the story will be told from your perspective, or point of view. This is called the first-person point of view, and it means that you should use the word "I" throughout your essay. Every detail should be relayed as *you* saw, felt, or experienced it. By writing narrative essays in the first person, it draws the reader in and makes it feel intimate, like you're sharing something very personal with only that reader.

DETAILS MAKE A STORY COME TO LIFE

Now that you know *how* to relay the details of your narrative (in the first person), let's talk about *what types* of details to relay. The details you include should cover the five Ws: who, what, where, when, and why. These kinds of details help put the story in context for the reader. The reader needs to know these basics or the story won't make much sense. Tell the reader who is involved, where and when the story is set, what happened or is happening, and why it happened.

You should also include sensory details in your narrative essay. Sensory details are the ones you perceive through your five senses. Let your reader know what was seen, heard, felt, smelled, and tasted. If the classroom was bright, say so. If the hallway stunk of old sneakers, clue in your reader to that. If the final bell sounded more like a foghorn, it pays to share!

It is also imperative to express how you feel emotionally about your topic. Were you worried, sad, anxious, excited, or giddy? Illustrate these feelings for your reader!

In short, lots of details bring the reader one step closer to actually being there.

USE STRONG LANGUAGE IN YOUR NARRATIVE ESSAY

Colorful, vibrant language will make your writing stand out, so be aware of using it in all of your writing assignments. Using active verbs is one way to do this. Active verbs are ones that depict action. Some verbs are "to be" verbs, such as were, is, was, and are. These are very ordinary. You can do better than ordinary! Use verbs with some flair to make your work feel lively. Also keep verbs close to the subject of the sentence to show more action, like this:

Chef la Fleur is an exceptional cook. Boring.
Chef la Fleur cooks exceptionally. Better!

Adverbs can help you better describe the action in your story because they modify verbs, which are action words. The chef in the example above doesn't just cook, he cooks exceptionally!

Use specific nouns in your essay, too. You didn't just go to school. Tell your reader you went to John F. Kennedy Junior High School. It wasn't simply a test; it was a geometry test. The dinner wasn't plain old steak and potatoes; it was filet mignon with roasted red potatoes!

Adjectives modify nouns and they can kick your narrative up a notch, too. Season your story with adjectives, but avoid using the most common ones, such as good, bad, pretty, and nice.

It was a hot day. Boring.
It was a sweltering day. Better!

Makes you long for air conditioning, doesn't it?

NARRATIVE ESSAY REVISION CHECKLIST

The draft is done, but the work needed to make your narrative essay stellar is not. You have to revise that work of genius first! Don't try to skip out on this part, or your essay will come across as a shabby and weak effort. There's a super-detailed guide to revising the content of your essay at the beginning of this book, but here's a checklist to get you started:

- ____ Does my introduction contain a solid thesis sentence?
- ____ Does my essay pass on an idea or feeling?
- ____ Does the essay lay out the plot in a clear and organized way?
- ____ Did I write my narrative in the first person?
- ____ Have I included enough details to make the reader feel like he or she was there, too?
- ____ Did I incorporate strong verbs, specific nouns, adjectives, and adverbs to enhance my writing?
- ____ Does my conclusion restate the point of my narrative essay and leave the reader thinking about a universal human experience?
- ____ Have I checked my essay for grammar, punctuation, and spelling errors?

WRITING A NARRATIVE ESSAY FOR A TEST

Writing essays in a test situation is a little different from writing one for a homework assignment. But, it's no reason to bolt out of the classroom! You now know a lot about narrative essays, so you're already well prepared. Now just follow these hints to write this type of essay on a test.

DECIPHER THE QUESTION

Reading directions is important on all tests. It's important with essay questions, too. Sometimes it's not completely obvious what type of essay you need to write. Look for certain words to let you know that a narrative is what's required. A narrative essay question could simply say: "Narrate a story about X." Narrative essay questions could also ask you to "describe" or "illustrate" a story about yourself.

BE AWARE OF TIME

There's nothing that you know more about than yourself, but that doesn't mean narrative essays take less time to write than other types of essays! You are allotted a certain amount of time to answer your narrative essay question, so get moving!

USE YOUR HEAD

During tests, you can't go out into the world to do direct observations, or do things like flip through photo albums and hope chests to recall memories. You'll have to rely on what's already stored in your memory! So think back to important events in your life and draw from your memory of those events.

TAKE THE STEPS

Follow the steps you learned about writing narrative essays earlier in this section. First, establish the main idea of your answer. Then, write a brief outline and draft your essay. Finally, reread your answer for flow and grammar. When rereading your answer, make sure your story has a good plot and reflects the human experience. Use tons of details, vivid language choices, and a first-person perspective.

SAMPLE NARRATIVE ESSAY

Here is a sample of a narrative essay using the topic outlined earlier in this chapter.

setting

character

When I was in the seventh grade, Pedro Martinez started attending my school. I never expected to be friends with the "new kid," let alone learn anything from him, but that's just what happened.

Thesis sentence

active verb

The bell for third period was clanging and I dodged into the locker room just in time. I quickly changed into my grubby lacrosse shorts and a T-shirt, laced up my Pumas, and headed into the gymnasium for class. That's when I spotted Pedro standing in the back of the group staring at his shoelaces as the other kids grabbed floor hockey sticks from a mesh bag and began horsing around with them. When we started the game, I moved nimbly around the gym, making dead-on passes, and scoring goal after goal. This was my game. But Pedro didn't even seem to know how to hold the stick. He seemed like my polar opposite and I thought, *We have nothing in common.*

specific noun

first person

That's why I was shocked when he approached me after class and asked if I could teach him to play. He commented on how good I was at floor hockey and looked at me with apprehension and excitement. I'm a sucker for a compliment, so I agreed. For the next few days I spent about half an hour teaching Pedro how to play floor hockey in the gym before the basketball team came in to take over the space. I taught him how to stick handle, how to shoot, and how to pass. Pedro was a quick study, and to everyone's surprise but my own, he scored a goal in gym class the following week. I was the first to slap him five.

details

That day, Pedro intercepted me as I was heading out of the locker room. His face grew a little red and he couldn't make eye contact with me. But he was able to squelch out the words thank you, and then added that he'd overheard me tell a friend I was struggling in Spanish class. This time, it was my face that grew a little red. I was having a hard time in Spanish class, and Pedro had just offered to tutor me.

So, for the next two weeks, Pedro and I spent study hall working on Spanish together. His parents even invited me to dinner one night. We inhaled his mother's empanadas and laughed together.

specific noun

Pedro and I are now the closest of friends, something I never anticipated when shy, seemingly unathletic Pedro showed up in my gym class that day. But sometimes you find friendship in unexpected places, at unexpected times. And if you're really lucky, you even come out of it with an A in Spanish class.

human experience

CHAPTER 5

PERSUASIVE ESSAYS

You've been assigned to write a persuasive essay. You got a major refresher on essays in general in the first section of this book, but what's with this "persuasive" business? *Persuasive* means to move by argument or request. You aren't going to argue as in yell and fight, though! Writing a persuasive essay is all about having an opinion. Your job is to convince others to agree with your opinion or to influence them to take a certain course of action.

If you are like most people, you have pretty strong opinions: Hamburgers are great, and so are the Yankees, but the Red Sox are the pits, and so is broccoli. Or maybe you feel that reading rules, but sports stink. Perhaps you think that people shouldn't eat red meat but that fish is okay. Everyone has thoughts and ideas about the world and the things in it. A persuasive essay is your chance to tell your reader what you think and why you think it—the main goal being that you want the reader to agree!

You've probably already put your powers of persuasion to good use in your daily life (but you may not have realized it without the fancy word attached!). Think about it: You want to go to the mall. Your parents don't think it's such a great idea. You disagree and you tell them why. You explain that you have a ride to and from with a responsible driver, that you cannot get into trouble there, and that you will call them periodically to check in while you are at the mall. Seems hard to argue with that, doesn't it? You've successfully persuaded them into letting you go!

Okay, but what does all this mean in terms of the persuasive essay assignment you've just received? It should be a piece of cake. Seriously! You persuade people all the time, so putting it on paper is no biggie. Let's get down to it, already.

ALLOW YOURSELF ENOUGH TIME TO WRITE YOUR PERSUASIVE ESSAY

When trying to figure out how much time to set aside for your persuasive essay writing assignment, keep the following steps in mind. They cannot be avoided or skipped if you want a successful essay when you're finished. Also make sure to factor in all of the other activities in your life. It's important to schedule enough time to write your persuasive essay.

PREWRITING

Start your assignment by choosing a topic, unless one has been chosen for you. Many persuasive essay topics will require you to do research so that you can back up your opinion with facts, statistics, and quotations from experts. Now is the time to do it! Then, make an opinion chart like the one on page 58. Finally, create an outline of the thoughts, facts, and ideas to be included in your essay.

WRITING

This is the stage at which you create a first draft of your essay. Your first draft should include an introduction, a body, and a conclusion. Try to use qualifying terms and even concede the point a little bit. (We'll get into this in greater detail later in this chapter.)

REVISING

Time to read your draft several times, and change it until you are completely satisfied. Have you actually convinced the reader by including supporting details, facts, etc.? Does your writing flow, and are your ideas well organized? The revision step is your chance to fix all of that.

EDITING AND PROOFREADING

Now you should go back and fix any spelling and grammar mistakes in your essay. Bad grammar and spelling will definitely affect your grade, even if your essay is incredible.

PRESENTING

Take the extra time to ensure that your paper looks nice. You can add charts or graphs to your persuasive essay. Things like this serve to further prove your point or opinion, and they show your teacher that you really put some effort into your assignment!

THE TOPIC OF YOUR PERSUASIVE ESSAY

First things first: You have to decide on the topic about which you'll write your persuasive essay (unless your teacher assigned a specific one, in which case you can skip right to the next section). If you have been left to your own devices, you are probably staring into space right now with no clue how to think of something to write about. Snap out of it! Here's some help.

BRAINSTORM

A great way to begin thinking of topics for your persuasive essay is to brainstorm. Brainstormed ideas are not good or bad, they're just ideas. So jot them down when they come to you. When you are done, you'll have a lot of material with which to work. At least a few of those brainstorms will probably make a perfect persuasive essay topic.

SURF THE WEB

The Internet is a portal to information about, well . . . everything. If it exists, you can probably find out more about it on the web! You can check out general news sites, and even online encyclopedias like Encyclopedia.com.

SCAN THE LIBRARY OR BOOKSTORE SHELVES

An additional way to come up with an essay topic is to head to your local bookseller or library. Walk the aisles and scan the books that seem interesting to you. It'll get the wheels turning.

REFER TO YOUR WRITER'S NOTEBOOK

You can use a journal or writer's notebook to record your dreams, jokes you hear, and even random thoughts and experiences. You can look back at these snippets of writing for a persuasive essay topic when one is needed. Plus, writing in your spare time will help you develop great writing skills!

OTHER THINGS TO KEEP IN MIND WHEN PICKING A TOPIC

The whole point of a persuasive essay is to sway the reader's opinion. The most important aspect of your topic is that it be something about which you feel strongly. Your opinions cannot come across as wishy-washy, so pick something that gets your blood boiling or something that gets your adrenaline pumping; something that makes you weepy or something that makes you feel joyous.

CHOOSE A PERSUASIVE ESSAY TOPIC THAT YOU CAN BACK UP

We'll discuss this in more detail later in this chapter, but before you choose a topic, remember one thing: You'll need to back it up. In a persuasive essay, you need to support your opinions with very strong reasons and details. These details and reasons help convince your reader that you're right. Think about how frustrating it is to have a conversation with someone who is trying to persuade you but has nothing solid with which to support his or her beliefs. Here is an example of an opinion with no factual support:

> "Michael Jordan was the best basketball player ever, just because. Trust me, he was."

This sentence doesn't tell the reader much at all, aside from the fact that the author likes Michael Jordan. You must tell the reader *why* with concrete reasons, like this:

> "Michael Jordan was the best basketball player ever because he was the NBA's Most Valuable Player five times, and he was an All-NBA First Team selection ten times."

In this sentence, the reader learns facts about Michael Jordan. These facts strongly support the argument that he is the best basketball player. This is where the persuasion part comes in! Filling your persuasive essay with facts, details, and examples that directly relate to your point makes the reader think, *Good point*, or *I see where you're coming from.*

ORGANIZE YOUR IDEAS

It's time to get organized! You may wonder if it's really important to organize your ideas before writing, and the answer is *yes!* You cannot put your thoughts to paper without first planning how you will map out your essay. Here are some helpful ways to organize before you begin writing.

GRAPHIC ORGANIZERS: MAKE AN OPINION CHART FOR A PERSUASIVE ESSAY

An opinion chart is a drawing in which you write down thoughts and feelings about your topic. Start by writing your opinion at the top of a blank page. Then make a chart with four columns and four rows. In the first column, write down each of the main reasons for your opinion. In each column to the right of that reason, write a supporting detail. Like this:

Opinion: The Beach Is the Best Place to Vacation			
Main Reasons for My Opinion	**Supporting Detail #1**	**Supporting Detail #2**	**Supporting Detail #3**
spend time outdoors	swimming	flying kites	building sand castles
relaxing	lying in the sun	reading	listening to water
plenty to do	miniature golf	boardwalk	go-cart track

WRITE AN OUTLINE

Outlines are a vital step in any piece of writing. They allow you to collect the many thoughts and ideas you have floating around in your head so that they can actually make sense to someone else.

Start by writing your thesis sentence on the top of the page under the introduction portion of the outline. A thesis sentence tells the reader the topic of the essay and what your opinion of that topic is.

Introduction
Opinion: I do not think that the school system should extend the length of the school day.

Then, write down at least three strong arguments toward that point, leaving space below each to add a little bit of detail. (You have to back it up, remember?)

I. Less time for after-school activities
   A. Clubs and organizations would suffer
   B. Outdoor sports teams would suffer

II. Less time to do assignments and study
   A. Less time to do homework before bedtime
   B. Students need time to study and practice at home what they heard in school to actually learn it well

III. Less family and friend time
   A. Kids need to interact with their friends
   B. Kids need time to spend with their families

Then add the conclusion portion of the outline. Restate your opinion and indicate what you want others to do about it.

Conclusion
Restate opinion: The school day should not be made longer.
Call to action: I think that students should go to the upcoming school board meeting and tell them not to make school longer.

Congratulations, you have yourself an outline! Feels good, doesn't it? It should, because you already have a lot of the work done.

WRITING THE FIRST DRAFT OF YOUR PERSUASIVE ESSAY

Utilize your outline in order to help you get your first draft in motion. The key to writing the first draft of any piece of writing is to get it over with—seriously! In film and television, actors get as many takes as they need to get it right, and so do you. Think of your persuasive essay draft as Take One! Just get the words on the page. You'll have plenty of opportunities to fine-tune it later. If you sit agonizing over every word and sentence at this stage in the game, you'll run out of steam pretty quickly.

THE PARTS OF A PERSUASIVE ESSAY

Let's get down to the nitty-gritty of a persuasive essay. All essays have three main components: an introduction, a body, and a conclusion. In a persuasive essay, each of these parts should serve to further prove your point, or whatever it is that you are trying to persuade. Everyone likes to believe that their opinions are right, but not all people will actually agree with you, so you have to convince them to in *every* part of the essay. Don't let a word go to waste!

In the introduction of a persuasive essay, you should state your argument or belief in a clear thesis sentence. You're telling the reader your opinion, so say it assertively. If you've chosen a topic that you really believe in, this should be pretty easy to do. Remember that your reader isn't psychic, so give a little bit of background information about the topic to let your reader know what you're talking about before he or she dives into your masterpiece.

> Having a dog as a pet is a great way to enrich your life. Dogs are truly man's best friend. But I feel that small dogs make better pets than large dogs.

The body of your persuasive essay should have at least three paragraphs. Each body paragraph should be focused on a different reason that supports your main opinion. Your strongest reason for the opinion you are arguing should appear in either the first or last body paragraph. This is so that you either begin the essay with a bang or end it with one. Both have a similar effect on the reader: making a lasting impression.

> The main reason that I feel small dogs make better pets than large dogs is because they are more practical for travel. Small dogs can travel with you much more easily than large dogs. They can be brought onboard airplanes and fly in a carrier under your seat. They can be put in a small bag and taken on errands. Also, small dogs can be brought in the car and still leave plenty of room for passengers.

Finally, the conclusion of a persuasive essay should wrap things up. The conclusion paragraph should always restate your central belief or opinion and then review the supporting reasons you discussed in the body of the essay. It can also include a final thought or idea about the topic that furthers your argument.

For an essay on small dogs, a conclusion could be like the following:

> As I've discussed, small dogs really do make better pets than large dogs. Small dogs are easier to travel with. Many small dog breeds shed and bark very little. It is also easier to bond and connect with small dogs because they can be picked up and held.

If you are trying to sway the reader to actually do something—to take some course of action—then, your conclusion should indicate what you'd like the reader to do. For example, your persuasive essay may be about the fact that you think soap and similar products should not be tested on animals. In the conclusion paragraph, let your reader know that they should write to the companies that do this urging them to stop.

SUPPORTING YOUR OPINION

Houses aren't built on toothpicks, and neither should your persuasive essay be. You have to give it a strong, solid foundation if it's actually going to *be* persuasive. As mentioned earlier in this chapter, you have to back it up with concrete reasons and examples.

LOOK IT UP

You're no doubt familiar with the Internet, so use it to your advantage. Look up your persuasive essay topic online to get more facts about it. Be wary of nonscholarly websites. If you are going to pull info from the web, be certain the site is well researched and accurate. Adding incorrect details to your essay is a surefire way *not* to persuade your reader that your opinion holds up. Here is an example of how factual details can add to your essay:

> Partially due to poaching, the giant panda is an endangered species.

OFFER STATISTICS

A good way to help support the opinion you're stating in a persuasive essay is to give cold, hard stats. For example:

> The town water supply can give enough water to 5,500 homes. The new housing development will add another 400 homes to the area.

INCLUDE YOUR OWN OBSERVATIONS

Another good way to back up your beliefs is to give your reader firsthand observations. Go see something for yourself so that you can write about it in an educated way.

> In our town, most people drive large SUVs.

ASK THE EXPERTS

When in doubt, go straight to the experts for information that will support your opinion. Having a knowledgeable person speak to your topic is a nice way to add seriousness and importance to your essay.

> According to the music teacher Ms. Kannry, students are more excited about the after-school music program than ever before.

MAKE YOUR ARGUMENT MORE BELIEVABLE

There are certain words and phrases you can use to make your persuasive essay more likely to, well . . . persuade. Use some of the statements below to help qualify your argument a little bit. When you qualify an opinion, you are softening it or limiting it. Why do you want to soften your argument? Well, because no one likes a know-it-all! If you march into your essay saying things like *always*, *never*, *in every case*, or *all of the time,* people are likely to disagree with you. Things are rarely cut-and-dried, good and bad, or right and wrong. There are a lot of gray areas in the world! It makes your opinion easier to support if you simply acknowledge that from the get-go.

Use these qualifying terms (ones that soften or limit your opinion) and you'll have your reader convinced in no time:

In many cases	Probably	Often
Usually	Much of the time	Almost
Frequently	Perhaps	Maybe
Most	Some	Almost

Another way to make the opinion expressed in a persuasive essay easy for a reader to accept is by conceding the point. When you concede something, it means that you are admitting that you do see the possible truth in opposite opinions.

You are more than likely thinking, *But, I thought the whole idea was to convince the reader that* I'm *right*! That is the point, and though arguing for the other side may sound like the complete opposite of what you should do, it works! It helps to make your argument more convincing when you show the reader that you are looking at the issue from both sides.

Here are a few phrases you can use in your persuasive essay to let the reader know that you see the subject from every angle:

I agree that . . . is also true.
I cannot argue with the fact that . . .
Admittedly . . .
I do see that . . . is possible.

PERSUASIVE ESSAY REVISION CHECKLIST

We all think that we got it right the first time, but the truth is that we rarely do. This rule applies to your persuasive essay, too. Repeat these words: I must reread and rewrite my writing. I must reread and rewrite my writing. One more time! I must reread and rewrite my writing! Then, use this checklist to make sure you hit all the high points of a top-notch persuasive essay:

____ Does my introduction contain a strong, opinionated thesis statement?
____ Does my introduction give the reader some background information about the topic I discuss in the rest of the essay?

____ Did I include at least three very strong reasons that support my opinion, with each point in a new paragraph?
____ Did I back up my reasons with details, facts, expert opinions, observations, and/or statistics?
____ Have I used qualifying terms and phrases to help make my argument easier to believe?
____ Have I shown both sides of the argument to make my point more convincing?
____ Does my conclusion restate my opinion and summarize the supporting reasons for that opinion?
____ Does my conclusion state a clear course of action for the reader to take, if applicable to the topic?
____ Have I checked my persuasive essay for grammar, punctuation, and spelling errors?

WRITING A PERSUASIVE ESSAY FOR A TEST

It's going to be nearly impossible to escape school without ever having to write an essay on a test. But don't worry! It's really nothing to be afraid of. You learned a lot about persuasive essays in this chapter, so now all you have to do is use those skills in the classroom. Here are some helpful tips:

DECIPHER THE QUESTION

Read the test question carefully to be sure you understand what type of essay you need to write. Test writers and teachers like to throw you for a loop once in a while by making questions seem trickier than they actually are. Look for certain clue words to let you know that you need to write a persuasive essay. Some persuasive essay questions will be very straightforward, and just ask you to "Persuade your reader of X" or "State your opinion about XYZ."

Other ways that a persuasive essay question may be posed are:

"Argue for or against Y."
"Convince a reader of XYZ."
"Prove that Z is the correct choice/opinion."
"Encourage others to agree with X."

BE AWARE OF TIME

Unlike a take-home essay, you need to get a test essay written in a very limited period of time. So get started as soon as you understand the question. Don't waste time dillydallying!

USE YOUR HEAD

Persuasive essays often require research so that you can support your opinion. But it's unlikely that you'll be able to leave the classroom and head to the Internet or library in the middle of a test! Be prepared to draw your supporting information from your very own brain.

TAKE THE STEPS

Follow the steps you learned about writing persuasive essays in this chapter. First, decide what your opinion is. Then, write a brief outline and draft your essay. Finally, reread your answer to check for grammar, punctuation, etc. And, of course, make sure that you have written a convincing argument about your point!

SAMPLE PERSUASIVE ESSAY

Here is a sample of a persuasive essay using the topic outlined earlier in this chapter.

Recently, the Monroe school board suggested that the length of school days be increased.	background information
This would mean that school would begin at 7:30 AM and end at 4 PM, rather than 2:15 PM, as it currently does. I do not think that the school system should extend the length of the school day.	thesis sentence with opinion
Extending the length of the school day would mean that there would be much less time for after-school activities. After-school activities such as drama club are important.	first supporting reason
They are fun and educational, and as Ms. Baldwin, the music teacher, says, "They help keep kids out of trouble after school."	expert testimony
But, if the school day was made longer, clubs and organizations would probably suffer.	qualifying term
Many kids wouldn't be able to stay at school even later than they do now. Some parents might not want their children coming home so late in the day,	qualifying term
and many students may not have a way to get home if the current schedule changes. In addition, outdoor sports teams would suffer because they would not have enough time to practice before dark.	supporting detail
A second reason that I feel the school day should not be made longer is that it would allow students less time to do assignments and study.	second supporting reason
Getting home later from school would mean that students have less time to do homework before bed. Students need this time to practice at home to reinforce what they learn in school.	supporting detail
Mr. Felix, the math teacher, says, "I find that students who complete all their homework do much better on exams."	expert testimony
A third reason I think that the school day should continue to end at 2:15 PM is that longer school days would mean students would have less time to spend with family and friends. Kids need to time interact with their friends to develop social skills.	third supporting reason
For most kids, it's important to	qualifying term

have time with friends to unwind after working hard in school all day, too. A parent of an eighth grader says, "Children also need to have time to spend with their families to keep the family bond strong." A longer school day would prohibit this.

supporting details

expert testimony

I feel very strongly that the Monroe school district should not make the school days end later than they currently do. I believe that lengthening school days will negatively affect many things that are important in a child's life: after-school programs, academics, and socialization. I think that students should go to the upcoming Monroe school board meeting and encourage them not to lengthen the school day.

restate the opinion

call to action

CHAPTER 6

HOW TO RESEARCH

Regardless of the type of essay you are writing, there's a pretty good chance that you'll have to research your topic first. So what exactly *is* research? And what's involved? Well, that depends on what you want to learn or understand. In general, research is the process of discovering facts and information. Research allows you to better understand any given topic. If you don't understand your topic, you won't have much to say about it. While research may seem like an extra step in the process of writing an essay, it's a necessary one.

SOURCES ARE YOUR SOURCE FOR INFORMATION

Research requires you to find sources. A source is nothing more than a place from which to draw information. Books are an old standby for getting the goods, but there are many options available to you. Let's take a closer look at different kinds of sources.

BOOKS

Books are often the best source of information when researching a topic. In the reference section of the library or bookstore, you'll find research books such as encyclopedias, dictionaries, and atlases. In other parts of the library or bookstore, you can find books specific to your topic, such as biographies, histories of a time or place, or books about animals or wars.

PERIODICALS

Periodicals are newspapers and magazines. The periodicals section of the library has titles such as *The New York Times*, *Newsweek*, and *National Geographic*. These types of publications can be very useful when researching an essay.

FILMS AND TELEVISION

Documentary and nonfiction films and TV programs about your topic are also great sources of information. Check out networks such as the History Channel, Animal Planet, and the Travel Channel.

THE INTERNET

If you have access to the World Wide Web at home or at school, you will find that it contains more sources of information than you can possibly count. You'll need a parent or teacher to help you pull information from only the best sites. Remember, not every website is a reputable source.

THE LESS OBVIOUS

Some unexpected sources for information might also include photo albums, family trees, old diaries or journals, and people. Yes, people! People hold a wealth of information and make fantastic sources. A for way to use a person as a source is through an interview. An interview is a conversation between two or mo people (the interviewer and the interviewee(s)). In an interview, the interviewer (that's you!) asks questions, and the interviewee answers them. The goal is to obtain information from the interviewee.

PRIMARY SOURCES VS. SECONDARY SOURCES

There are two major kinds of sources: primary and secondary. *Primary* is a word meaning "first," while *secondary* means "second." If you expand on that, understanding the differences between them isn't very complicated.

Ever play telephone or grapevine when you were little? In that game, the first person in the chain tells the second person something. The second person tells the third person the same fact. The third tells the fourth, and so on. By the end of the telephone chain or vine, the message is always muddled, isn't it? That's the fun of the game—to see how different the message is from the beginning to the end! But in research, good sources give a clear message, not a muddled one.

A primary source can be linked straight to its author, without anyone in between. In the telephone game, the primary source is the person who started the chain. Primary sources simply report the facts without the interpretation of anyone. They are original sources, meaning the information is coming straight from the horse's mouth.

Secondary sources take information from primary sources and restate it. The second, third, and fourth person (and everyone after them) in a telephone chain are secondary sources. The information is secondhand. Or thirdhand or fourthhand . . . Those sources can sometimes muddle up the message, like in the game. That's why many teachers and scholars prefer primary sources, if they're available.

TYPES OF PRIMARY SOURCES

Primary sources provide firsthand information or knowledge. Here are some ideas for places to find primary sources for your research.

INTERVIEWS

Interviews can be an invaluable primary source. Generally, experts in the subject about which you are writing are your best bet. Interviews with people who lived through an experience or time period are equally great. For example, if you are writing an essay about a major change at your school, you should interview the principal, teachers, or other students. Or, if your essay assignment is to write a personal narrative about a childhood memory, you should interview a grandparent, parent, or sibling—someone who remembers being there, too. The other perk about doing interviews is that you can use direct quotations in your essay. Direct quotations will make your essay seem very professional. That's always a good route to securing an A!

AUTOBIOGRAPHIES

Autobiographies are another example of a primary source. The term comes from the Greek words *auto*, meaning "self," *bios*, meaning "life," and *graphein*, meaning "write." An autobiography is a biography about the author! You're getting the author's life story, or at least a part of it, in his or her own words.

DIARY OR JOURNAL ENTRIES

A diary or journal is a book in which a person writes about his or her life over the course of time. But diaries are different from autobiographies. Diaries aren't meant for anyone else to read, unlike autobiographies, which are. Usually diaries are dated and written chronologically. People often share secrets and feelings in diaries. That's why they make such great primary sources!

DIRECT OBSERVATION

Another good way to research your essay is to give your reader firsthand observations. Go see it for yourself! Or even better, do it yourself. For example, if your essay is about white tigers, go observe them yourself at the zoo. Maybe your essay is about baseball. Go down to the park with some friends and play ball! It'll make your essay that much better.

TYPES OF SECONDARY SOURCES

Secondary sources are created by someone who was not actually there. Secondary sources often include the opinions of the author. Most books, articles, and Internet sites are secondary sources, but here are some specific ones.

ENCYCLOPEDIAS

An encyclopedia is a collection of information about a large amount of topics. Encyclopedias are written by experts and are most often in book form, but nowadays, they are online as well. There are general encyclopedias, such as World Book and Britannica. These types of encyclopedias offer short entries about just about anything you can think of—from dogs to photosynthesis; George Washington to forensics. There are also encyclopedias that are a bit more focused, such as medical encyclopedias, legal encyclopedias, or ones about American history, plants, and animals.

BIOGRAPHIES

Biographies are books written about a person's life, but they are written by someone else. Good biographies are written with the approval of the subject (or the family of the subject, if the person has died) and are very well researched by the author.

USING THE INTERNET FOR RESEARCH

The Internet can be very valuable when researching your essay topic. You don't even have to leave your house or school to have endless amounts of information at your fingertips.

A surefire way to locate Internet sites that are suitable for your essay is to use kid-friendly search engines. A search engine is an Internet tool that collects all of the sites available on the Web and sorts them in order of relevance to your topic. They find as many sites as possible that have to do with your subject. Examples of search engines include Google.com and Ask.com.

SEARCH ENGINES FOR KIDS

There are some search engines designed especially for students. They eliminate sites that are not age-appropriate or that aren't really relevant to topics for which a student would search. The following is a list of some good student-friendly search engines. Start your Internet research by using one of them, rather than a general search engine, and you'll save yourself time!

AOL @ School: www.aolatschool.com
Ask Jeeves Kids: www.ajkids.com
CyberSleuth Kids: www.cybersleuth-kids.com
Family Friendly Search: www.familyfriendlysearch.com
KidsClick!: www.kidsclick.org
Yahoo Kids: www.yahooligans.com

While the Internet seems like the easiest and most effective way to get info, be wary of it. Internet sites are not all created equal. Anyone can post information on the web, but it doesn't mean that it is all valid or even true. Stick to well-known, scholarly sites to be sure the information you are obtaining is accurate. Your parents, teachers, and librarians can help you determine which sites are trustworthy.

Another thing to be aware of when using the Internet for research is that websites disappear. One day they are there, and the next, poof—they're gone! That's why it's a wise idea to print out web pages from which you are obtaining information you're using in your essay. Another option is to save the page to a CD as a text or source file. That way, if the site gets removed from the web, you can still access the information and give credit to the source.

TAKING INFORMATION FROM SOURCES

Regardless of the type of sources you opt to use, you will have to take good notes on your research to properly apply it to your essay. The best way to do this is to have a package of index cards at the ready. You'll use a bunch of them. (Don't worry, you're only putting a sentence or phrase on each!) Consult all of your sources and write down the most important pieces of information each one offers about your topic. Then place them in the order you want the information to appear in the essay.

Before you dive into note taking, you need to make source cards. (More cards? Yes, but only a few!) Source cards keep you organized as you take notes. Write the name of each of your sources on an index card, along with its author, and then assign the source a number. Write that number in the top right-hand corner of its index card. Here are a few examples of source cards for an essay about dogs:

#1

Puppies for Dummies: A Reference for the Rest of Us.
Sarah Hodgson.

#2

The Shih Tzu Handbook. Sharon L. Vanderlip, D.V.M.

#3

Bow the Dog. Universe Publishing.

Now every time you take a note from *Puppies for Dummies*, mark a #1 on that card, so that you know the information came from that source. Every time you take a note from *Bow the Dog,* mark a #3 on the card, and so on. This allows you to keep track of what information came from where, and it's much faster than writing out the entire source title every time you take a new note.

So, what's the point of keeping track of your sources? The point is to give them credit later. Any piece of information used in your essay that is taken from a source, no matter how small or insignificant it may seem, didn't originate from you. So, you'll need to list its source in your bibliography or works cited page.

(Flip forward to page 72 for an explanation of bibliographies and works cited pages.)

Another reason to take notes and make source cards is to avoid plagiarism. Plagiarism is when you use information or a quote and pass it off as your own. It's simply never acceptable to copy information word-for-word from a source and reuse it exactly the same way in your essay without giving proper credit. When writing research-based essays, it is often tempting to do this because it seems like less work for you. Avoid the temptation, though! Not only is plagiarizing cheating, it's also illegal. No joke!

It is easy to avoid accidentally plagiarizing if you follow the proper note-taking guidelines. Do not copy information from your sources word-for-word. Write down only the most important parts of any statement. This will make the note-taking process go much more quickly, and it will prevent you from accidentally copying the author's exact words.

When you write your first draft, use the facts you noted, but rephrase them *in your own words*. Your voice is the one your teacher must be reading on the page, not the voice of the author of the source.

Here are a few sample note cards for an essay about dogs:

#3
Beagles are one of the all-time most popular breeds in U.S.

#1
There are seven standard dog breed groups: sporting, hound, working, herding, terrier, nonsporting, and toy.

#2
Shih Tzu is an example of a toy breed.

Okay, but what if you want to use a quote from a source? You can do that, but you must put the text inside quotation marks and make sure to credit the source. For example:

According to Sarah Hodgson, "Bred to follow scent, scent hounds are active, lively, and rugged."

COMMON KNOWLEDGE

Common knowledge is a term that describes information that is widely known. If a fact is common knowledge, you do not need to cite a source for it. This is an important distinction to understand because it can help you avoid plagiarizing. Here are some examples of common knowledge:

George Washington was the first president of the United States.

Albany is the capital of New York State.

Buttercup plants are yellow.

Britney Spears is a pop star.

Facts that most people do not know off the top of their heads are not common knowledge, and need to be credited in your essay. If you have any doubt about whether or not something is common knowledge, it's better to play it safe. Give credit where credit is due.

BIBLIOGRAPHIES AND WORKS CITED

A bibliography is an alphabetical list of all the sources you used or consulted to create a piece of writing. It should appear at the end of your essay and needs to be done very carefully. When creating a bibliography, list your sources (books, articles, interviews, and so on) in alphabetical order by authors' last names. Sources that don't have authors (encyclopedias, movies) should be alphabetized by title.

When you "cite" something, you are quoting it. A works cited page is basically the same thing as a bibliography. It's a place where you list the sources you used. There's one main difference between a bibliography and a works cited, however. A works cited contains only the sources from which you took direct quotations. Unlike a bibliography, it does not include all the sources you consulted, but rather only the ones you actually cited in your paper. Hence its name! Some teachers may ask for both a works cited page and a bibliography. If that's the case, the works cited page should appear at the end of your essay. The bibliography goes on another separate page and should appear after the works cited page.

Bibliographies and works cited pages have very specific punctuation that depends on the type of source you are listing. Your teacher should provide you with specific instructions for how your bibliography or works cited should look, but here are few general guidelines:

- Number each page. Continue the numbering from the last page of the text. Type your last name and the page number in the upper right-hand corner. Leave a half-inch margin at the top of the page.

- Center the word(s) "Bibliography" or "Works Cited" one inch from the top of the page. Double-space before the first entry.

- Type each entry in alphabetical order by the author's last name. If the source has no author, alphabetize by the first word of the title. If the words *A, An,* or *The* appear in the title, ignore them when deciding how to alphabetize.

- Begin each entry flush against the left margin. If an entry takes up more than one line, indent the additional lines a half-inch (or five spaces).

- Double-space the entire page (within each entry *and* between entries).

HOW TO CITE

Below are examples of types of sources done in a common style:

BOOKS

Author Last Name, Author First Name. Book Title. Publication Location: Publisher, Copyright Year.

MAGAZINES

Author Last Name, Author First Name. "Article Title." Publication Title. Month and Year of Publication Date: Page Number(s).

NEWSPAPERS

Author Last Name, Author First Name. "Article Title." Name of Newspaper [City] Day Month Year of Publication, Edition if available: Section and Page Number(s).

(Note that months should be abbreviated, except May, June, and July.)

ENCYCLOPEDIAS

Author Last Name, Author First Name (if available). "Article Title." Encyclopedia Name. Edition. Number of total volumes, place of pub: Pub, Year.

TV PROGRAMS

"Title of Episode." Title of Program. Name of Network. Call Letters, City of Local Station (if any). Broadcast Date.

FILMS

Title, Director. Distributor, Year.

CD-ROMS

Disc Title. Version. Place of Publication: Name of Publisher, Date of Publication.

PEOPLE (INTERVIEWS)

Last Name, First Name. Type of Interview. Date of Interview.

INTERNET (GENERAL)

Author Last Name, Author First Name. Article or Page Title. Date Assigned to the Site (if available). Institution or Organization affiliated with the Site (if available). Date You Accessed the Site for the Information<URL>.

INTERNET MESSAGES OR BOARDS

Author Last Name, Author First Name. "Subject of Message." Online posting. Date. Name of Forum. Date of Access [run in] Available e-mail: LISTSERV@ e-mail address.

You are now armed to begin researching any essay topic like a pro. Use this chapter as a reference tool throughout your assignments to be certain you're on the right track. Good luck!

CHAPTER 7

EDITING YOUR ESSAYS

Once you have brainstormed your idea, researched your topic, written a draft, and revised your draft, you are ready to edit your essay. Half of the revision process involves rereading for style and accuracy of facts. (See Chapter 1 for more extensive information about how to do this.) The other half of the revision process involves editing to check spelling, grammar, punctuation, tenses, and all the rest of that English mumbo jumbo that makes your head spin. Have no fear, your editing guide is here! This final chapter is a guide to help you edit any piece of writing. Use it as a reference tool when you are ready to edit your essays.

PROOFREADING MARKS

When professional editors proofread a piece of writing, they use a standard set of marks to do so. Use the following marks as you edit your essay.

Symbol	Meaning	Example
ℊ or ɤ or ⁊	delete	The brown sad dog sleeps. ɤ
⌒ ‿	close up	Don't with hold information. ⌒ ‿
ℊ̑	delete and close up	cloqse up ℊ̑
^ or > or ^	insert	insert ^ here word
#	insert a space	put onehere #
eq#	space evenly	space ^ evenly ^ where ^ indicated eq#
stet	let stand	let marked ~~text~~ stand as set stet
tr	transpose	change order the tr
/	used to separate two or more marks and often as a concluding stroke at the end of an insertion	The brown sad dogs sleeps^ ɤ/⊙
[	set farther to the left	[too far to the right
]	set farther to the right	too far to the left]
⌒	set as ligature (such as æ)	encyclopaedia
⌒	align horizontally	alignment

Symbol	Meaning	Example
//	align vertically	// align with surrounding text
x	broken character	imperfect x
⊓	indent or insert em quad space	list ⊓ em
¶	begin a new paragraph	¶ The brown dog sleeps.
(sp)	spell out	set (5 lbs.) as five pounds (sp)
cap	set in CAPITALS	set nato as NATO cap
sm cap or s.c.	set in SMALL CAPITALS	set signal as SIGNAL s.c.
lc	set in lowercase	set South as south lc
ital	set in *italic*	set oeuvre as *oeuvre* ital
rom	set in roman	Set as Times New Roman *Regular* rom
bf	set in **boldface**	Set as Times New Roman Bold bf
= or -/ or ⁀	hyphen	multi colored =
1/N or en or /N/	en dash	1965-72 1/N
1/M or em or /M/	em (or long) dash	Now—at last!-we know. 1/M
∨	superscript or superior	as in πr2 = as in πr^2
∧	subscript or inferior	as in H20 = as in $H_2 0$
◊ or ✕	centered	for centered dot in *p* *q*
∧,	comma	Trenton NJ
∨'	apostrophe	St. Johns is a hospital.
⊙	period	St. John's is a hospital ⊙
; or ;/	semicolon	Juan wants to visit his uncle, however, he has made no plans. ;/
: or ⊙	colon	The following ⊙
∨" ∨" or ∨' ∨'	quotation marks	This guy... Lucas said.
(/)	parentheses	—*Publishers Weekly* starred review (/)

Symbol	Meaning	Example
[/]	brackets	The AWF African Wildlife Foundation works to protect the wildlife in Africa. [/]
ok/?	query to author: has this been set as intended?	The waves were high that day. ok/?
(turn symbol)	turn over an inverted letter	inverted (turn symbol)
wf	wrong font	wrong siZe or style wf

SPELLING

Start the editing process by checking your spelling. If you have composed your essay on a computer, you can use the spell-check function as a first step to catch obvious errors. After that, you have to actually read each word with your own two eyes! There's no way around giving your essay a careful read for spelling, and here's the reason why: The spell-check function in word-processing programs only finds words that are not a part of the English language. For example, in your essay you might write, "I sea a stationary store." *See* anything wrong there? You meant to write *see*, not *sea*! And station*a*ry with an *a* means to stand still, while station*e*ry with an *e* means paper. These words are spelled correctly, but have different meanings from the ones that should have been used. Contrary to how it may seem, your computer does not have a brain and doesn't know which one you meant to write!

USING SUFFIXES

Many words come from a base word. Often, a suffix is placed after the base word to make new words from it. A suffix is a group of letters tacked onto the end of the base word in order to modify its meaning or change it into a different word.

Suffix	Meaning
-ful	full of
-ous	full of
-ly	like
-able	able to be
-ible	able to be
-er, -or	one who does
-less	without
-en	made of
-ish	like; resembling
-ment	act of
-ness	quality of

- When a base word ends with a silent *e*, and the suffix you want to add begins in a vowel, drop the *e* in the base word before adding the suffix.

  Like becomes *Likable*

  Exceptions include *knowledgeable*.

  BUT

  When a base word ends with a silent *e*, and the suffix you want to add begins with a consonant, do not drop the *e* in the base word before adding the suffix.

  Use becomes *Useful*

  Exceptions include *argument, judgment,* and *truly.*

- When a base word ends in *y* and is preceded by a consonant, change the *y* to *i* before adding a suffix (unless the suffix begins with *i*).

  Beauty becomes *Beautiful*

  BUT

  Cry becomes *Crying*

- When a one-syllable word ends in a consonant preceded by a single vowel, double the consonant before a suffix beginning with a vowel.

  Hit becomes *Hitting*

- When a word has more than one syllable, ends in a consonant preceded by a single vowel, has an accent on the last syllable, and the suffix begins with a vowel, you should still double the consonant. That's a mouthful, but here is an example:

Begin becomes *Beginner*

USING PREFIXES

Prefixes are letter groupings kind of like suffixes, but instead they create new words when added to the *beginning* of a base word. Here is a list of common prefixes and their meanings.

Prefix	Meaning
pre-	before
un-	not; opposite of
dis-	not; opposite of
in-	not
im-	not
il-	not
ir-	not
fore-	before
mis-	wrong
co-	together
re-	again; back

- When one of these prefixes is added to a word beginning with the same letter that the prefix ends in, there will be, for example, two *s*'s or *n*'s.

  Spell becomes *Misspell*

  Natural becomes *Unnatural*

- When one of these prefixes is added to a word that does not begin with the same letter that the prefix ends in, there will be, for example, only one *n* or *s*.

  Understand becomes *Misunderstand*

  Willing becomes *Unwilling*

I BEFORE E

When the letters *e* and *i* appear next to each other in a word, it's pretty confusing as to which one comes first. So don't feel disheartened if they trip you up from time to time. Some words are spelled with *ei*, such as *receive*. Some words are spelled with *ie*, such as *believe*. The general rule is that *i* comes before *e*, except after *c* or when it sounds like *a*, as in *neighbor* and *weigh*.

Here are a few exceptions to this rule:

ie after c: *science*, *sufficient*, *agencies*, *financier*

ei not after c: *their*, *foreign*, *being*, *neither*, *weird*, *vein*

If you have any doubts, put your dictionary to good use.

COMMONLY MISSPELLED WORDS

Here is a list of commonly misspelled words. You can refer to it if you're having trouble spelling a word.

absence
absorption
accommodate
ache
acquaintance
across
address
advice
again
ally
already
always
among
analysis
analyze
angel
angle
annual
answer
appetite
arctic
ascent
awkward
beginning
believe
benefit
bicycle

boundary
broccoli
bulletin
bureau
burglar
business
cafeteria
calendar
ceiling
cemetery
changeable
chocolate
colonel
column
coming
commercial
committee
confidence
conscientious
conscious
control
controversy
convertible
curiosity
dealt
decease
deceive

definite
descent
desperate
despise
develop
device
disastrous
discipline
doctor
ecstasy
eighth
embarrass
eminent
enough
envelope
environment
everything
exceed
exercise
existence
expedition
expense
extraordinary
familiar
fascinate
fasten
February

fiery
fluorescent
foreign
forfeit
forty
friend
fulfill
genius
government
governor
grammar
grateful
guarantee
guess
handsome
harass
height
history
hoarse
hour
humorous
immediately
independent
indispensable
innocent
interfere
introduce

jealous
jewelry
judgment
ketchup
knowledge
laboratory
legitimate
leisure
library
license
literature
magnificent
maintenance
mathematics
meant
medal
mediocre
millennium
millionaire
miniature
minute
miscellaneous
mischievous
misspell
mortgage
muscle
mysterious
mystery
necessary
neighbor
night
ninth
noticeable
nuclear
occasion
occurrence
often
omitted
optimistic
origin
original
pageant
perform
permanent
perseverance
picnicking
piece
pigeon
pleasant
possessive
prairie
precede
prejudice
principal
principle
privilege
professor
pumpkin
pursue
quantity
quiet
quite
raise
raspberry
receipt
receive
referred
reign
repeat
repetition
restaurant
rhyme
rhythm
ridiculous
sacrifice
schedule
science
scissors
secretary
seize
separate
siege
sincerely
special
specimen
stationery
strictly
succeed
sugar
superintendent
surgeon
sympathize
temporary
therefore
thorough
through
tomorrow
tragedy
truly
typical
until
vacuum
vegetable
vengeance
warrant
wear
Wednesday
week
weird
whether
which
whole
women
won't
would
writer
writing
written
wrote
you're

PARTS OF SPEECH

Adjective: a word that describes a noun or pronoun

tiny, flat, long

Adverb: a word that describes a verb, an adjective, or another adverb

Hint: often ends in –ly, like quickly

Conjunction: a word that connects other words

if, and, but, or

Interjection: a word that shows strong emotion and is set off by commas or an exclamation point

Eeek! Ouch!

Noun: a word that indicates a person, place, or thing

Madonna, school, video game

Preposition: a word that shows position or direction

above, near, by, on

A preposition can also introduce a prepositional phrase, such as *in the water.*

Pronoun: a word used in place of a noun

she, it, they

Verb: a word that shows action or links the subject to another word within the sentence

was, can, skate, run

CAPITALIZATION RULES

Capitalize the first word in a sentence:

__S__he was late to class.

Capitalize the pronoun *I*:

After breakfast, __I__ took a walk.

Capitalize proper nouns, which are the names of specific people, places, and things:

The chef's name is __S__hari __W__oods. She lives in __F__ort __L__auderdale.

Capitalize the days of the week and the months of the year:

__S__unday *__A__pril*

Capitalize official title or positions when they come in front of a person's name:

__D__r. Spock *__P__resident Bush*

Capitalize holidays, festivals, and special events:

__C__hristmas *__K__wanzaa* *__V__alentine's Day*

Capitalize the first word of a quotation:

Martin Luther King, Jr. said, "__L__et Freedom Ring."

Capitalize abbreviations of titles when they follow a person's name:

*Martin Luther King, **J**r* *Barry Glickman, **M.D**.*

Capitalize the first word in the greeting of a friendly letter:

***D**ear Melissa,* ***H**i, Shannon,*

Capitalize the first word and all the main words in the greeting of a business letter:

***T**o **W**hom **I**t **M**ay **C**oncern:*

***D**ear **S**ir or **M**adam:*

Capitalize the first word in the closing of any letter:

***B**est wishes,* ***M**uch love,*

Capitalize the names of languages:

***S**panish* ***F**rench*

Capitalize the names of family members when you are speaking directly to them, or when you are using their names:

***G**randpa Morris*

***M**om and **D**ad, this is my teacher.*

Capitalize all the main words in a book, movie, song, television show, magazine, or newspaper:

*Book: **H**arry **P**otter and the **G**oblet of **F**ire*

*Movie: **S**uperman **R**eturns*

*Song: "**W**hat a **W**onderful **W**orld"*

*Television show: **A**merican **I**dol*

*Magazine: **R**olling **S**tone*

*Newspaper: **T**he **N**ew **Y**ork **T**imes*

Capitalize religions, tribes, ethnicities, and nationalities:

***J**ewish* ***I**rish* ***I**roquois* ***I**slam*

Capitalize the names of all the planets:

***E**arth* ***M**ars*

Capitalize the names of historical periods and events:

***R**evolutionary **W**ar* ***A**ge of **E**nlightenment*

PUNCTUATION

Follow these guidelines for using each type of punctuation mark.

PERIOD

Use a period at the end of a sentence that states something:

I am late for class.

Use a period after abbreviations or initials in a name:

Mrs. P. Quigley

QUESTION MARK

Use a question mark at the end of a question:

Where are my shoes?

Use a question mark at the end of a declarative sentence that expresses the feeling, *I can't believe this!*

He won the spelling bee?

EXCLAMATION POINT

Use an exclamation point at the end of a sentence that expresses a strong emotion:

I'm mad at you!

Use an exclamation point after a *strong* interjection:

Wait! Don't leave without me.

APOSTROPHE

Use an apostrophe in a possessive noun:

The dog's bone is in his mouth.
My class's science fair project won.
The girls' soccer team won the game!

Use an apostrophe in a contraction to show where the missing letter or letters used to be:

It is = It's *We will = We'll*
She is = She's *I have = I've*

COMMA

Use a comma to separate the complete thoughts in a sentence:

I read a book about dogs, but Erik read a book about sports.

Use a comma between two adjectives when they describe the same noun:

The fat, old cat stretched out on the sofa.

Use a comma to separate items in a list:

We need milk, butter, and eggs to make the cake.

Use a comma to set off a quotation:

Kerrie said, "I have to read this book."

Use a comma to set apart interjections at the beginning of a sentence:

Wow, I'm tired.

Use a comma in the greeting and closing of a friendly letter:

Dear Maggie, *Best wishes,*

When writing the date, use a comma to separate the month and day from the year:

September 14, 1973

When writing an address, use a comma to separate the city and the state:

Brooklyn, New York

QUOTATION MARKS

Use quotation marks to show a person's words:

"Stay in line," the teacher said.

Use quotation marks to set off the names of songs, essays, articles, chapters in a book, poems, and speeches:

"I Have a Dream"

COLON

Use a colon in the greeting of a formal letter:

Dear Governor:

Use a colon to introduce lists:

We have to buy three things at the store: eggs, butter, and sugar.

When writing the time, use a colon to separate hours from minutes:

1:40 *12:00*

ELLIPSES

Ellipses are used to show that words have been left out of a sentence:

*Someone's been . . . in my bed. (Someone's been **sleeping** in my bed.)*

Ellipses are used to show that there is a pause in dialogue:

Why am I late? Well . . . um . . . something came up!

VERBS

VERB TENSES

Make sure to use the same verb tense throughout your piece of writing. *Tense* means "time." A verb's tense tells the reader when in time the action of the verb takes place.

Present tense means the action is taking place now:

***I bake** cookies.*

Past tense means the action took place before now:

***I baked** cookies.*

Future tense means the action has not happened yet, but will anytime after now:

***I will bake** cookies.*

Present perfect tense means the action started in the past but is still happening in the present:

***I have baked** cookies.*

Past perfect tense means the action started in the past and was finished in the past:

***I had baked** cookies.*

Future perfect tense means the action will start in the future and will be done at a specific time in the future:

***I will have baked** cookies.*

IRREGULAR VERBS

Verbs are changed to show tense: present, past, or past participle. Most verbs can be altered to show their past or past participle tense by adding *-ed* to their present form. But, there are also many verbs for which adding the *-ed* ending doesn't hold true. These are called irregular verbs. Here's a list of common ones, but if you're ever unsure, just look it up in the dictionary.

Present Form	Past Tense	Past Participle
am, be	was, were	been
awake	awoke	awoken
beat	beat	beaten
become	became	become
begin	began	begun
bend	bent	bent
bet	bet	bet
bite	bit	bitten
bleed	bled	bled
blow	blew	blown
break	broke	broken
bring	brought	brought
build	built	built
burn	burned/burnt	burned/burnt
burst	burst	burst
buy	bought	bought
catch	caught	caught
choose	chose	chosen
cling	clung	clung
come	came	come
cost	cost	cost
creep	crept	crept
cut	cut	cut
deal	dealt	dealt
dig	dug	dug
dive	dived/dove	dived
do	did	done
draw	drew	drawn
dream	dreamed/dreamt	dreamed/dreamt
drive	drove	driven
drink	drank	drunk
eat	ate	eaten
fall	fell	fallen
feed	fed	fed
feel	felt	felt
fight	fought	fought
find	found	found
fit	fit	fit

Present Form	Past Tense	Past Participle
fling	flung	flung
fly	flew	flown
forget	forgot	forgotten
forgive	forgave	forgiven
freeze	froze	frozen
get	got	gotten
give	gave	given
go	went	gone
grow	grew	grown
hang	hung	hung
hear	heard	heard
hide	hid	hidden
hit	hit	hit
hold	held	held
hurt	hurt	hurt
keep	kept	kept
kneel	knelt	knelt
know	knew	known
lay	laid	laid
lead	led	led
leap	leaped/lept	leaped/lept
learn	learned/learnt	learned/learnt
leave	left	left
lend	lent	lent
let	let	let
lie	lay	lain
light	lighted/lit	lighted
lose	lost	lost
make	made	made
mean	meant	meant
meet	met	met
mow	mowed	mowed/mown
overcome	overcame	overcome
pay	paid	paid
prove	proved	proved/proven
put	put	put
quit	quit	quit
read	read	read
ride	rode	ridden

Present Form	Past Tense	Past Participle
ring	rang	rung
rise	rose	risen
run	ran	run
saw	sawed	sawed/sawn
say	said	said
see	saw	seen
seek	sought	sought
sell	sold	sold
send	sent	sent
sew	sewed	sewed/sewn
shake	shook	shaken
shave	shaved	shaved/shaven
shine	shone	shone
shoe	shoed	shoed/shod
shoot	shot	shot
show	showed	showed/shown
shrink	shrank	shrunk
shut	shut	shut
sing	sang	sung
sink	sank	sunk
sit	sat	sat
sleep	slept	slept
slide	slid	slid
speak	spoke	spoken
speed	sped	sped
spend	spent	spent
spill	spilled/spilt	spilled/spilt
spin	spun	spun
split	split	split
spread	spread	spread
stand	stood	stood
steal	stole	stolen
stick	stuck	stuck
sting	stung	stung
stink	stank	stunk
strike	struck	struck
string	strung	strung
swear	swore	sworn
sweep	swept	swept

Present Form	Past Tense	Past Participle
swim	swam	swum
swing	swung	swung
take	took	taken
teach	taught	taught
tear	tore	torn
tell	told	told
think	thought	thought
thrive	thrived/throve	thrived
throw	threw	thrown
understand	understood	understood
upset	upset	upset
wake	woke	woken
wear	wore	worn
weave	weaved/wove	weaved/woven
weep	wept	wept
win	won	won
wind	wound	wound
write	wrote	written

SUBJECT-VERB AGREEMENT

As you probably know, the subject of a sentence tells you who or what the sentence is about. The verb tells you what the subject is doing or being. In a sentence, it's important that the subject and verb "match." This matching is called subject-verb agreement. Take a look at the following sentence: *The dog is barking.*

The subject is *dog*. The verb is *is*. *Dog* and *is* "match" because they are both singular. *Singular* means "one." Singular subjects go with singular verbs: *The dog barks. Plural* means "more than one." Plural subjects go with plural verbs: *The dogs bark.*

AVOIDING RUN-ON SENTENCES AND SENTENCE FRAGMENTS

When creating any piece of writing, you must avoid run-on sentences and sentence fragments. Run-on sentences are sentences in which two or more simple sentences are combined without the correct punctuation separating them. For example:

> She isn't prepared for the test she's going to get a bad grade.

To read properly, this sentence could be rewritten as follows:

> She isn't prepared for the test. She's going to get a bad grade.

Or even better:

She isn't prepared for the test, so she's going to get a bad grade.

A sentence fragment is formed when a sentence does not include either a subject or a verb and does not contain a complete thought. For example:

Are not my sneakers!

This sentence is missing a subject. To read properly, this sentence could be rewritten as follows:

They are not my sneakers!

Here is a sentence missing a subject and a verb:

On my way to school.

To read properly, this sentence could be rewritten as follows:

I am on my way to school.

HOMONYMS, HOMOGRAPHS, AND OTHER TRICKY WORDS

There are many words in the English language that sound similar but have different spellings and meanings. They are called *homonyms*. Other words are spelled the same, but have different pronunciations and meanings. They are called *homographs*. There are also groups of words, such as *can* and *may*, that are often mistakenly used for one another. The following is an extensive list that explains which word to use when!

Term/Definition	Example
accept: a verb meaning "to receive"	I accepted the award.
except: a preposition meaning "other than"	Everyone went to the party, except Sue.
affect: a verb meaning "to influence"	The storm affected our family.
effect: most often used as a noun meaning "the result"	The effects of the storm were widespread.
allowed: a verb meaning "permitted"	We are not allowed to play ball in the house.

Term/Definition	Example
aloud: an adverb meaning "in a normal speaking voice"	I read the poem aloud.
all ready: a phrase meaning "completely prepared"	I am all ready to go to the park.
already: an adverb meaning "previously"	We already went to the grocery store.
all right: a phrase meaning "satisfactory" or "very well" **alright:** a much less common way of spelling *all right.* It also means "satisfactory" or "very well."	I did all right on the test.
all together: a phrase meaning "gathered" or "at one time"	The chorus sang all together.
altogether: an adverb meaning "completely"	The team was altogether tired from running.
allusion: a reference to a person, place, or thing that is commonly known	I made an allusion to Goldilocks.
illusion: a false impression	The magician created an optical illusion.
a lot: a phrase that means "plenty." This is NOT spelled as one word.	We made a lot of cookies!
among: a preposition used to compare more than two things	The four girls talked among themselves.
between: a preposition used to compare exactly two things. It also means "from one to another."	I had to choose between going to the beach or going skiing.
ant: an insect	The ant carried a piece of bread.
aunt: a relative, usually the sister of a mother or father	My aunt gave me socks for my birthday.
bare: an adjective meaning "naked"	The baby's bottom was bare!
bear: a large mammal	The bear stole the honey.
base: the foundation or lower part of something	The ski lodge is at the base of the mountain.
bass [sounds like *mass*]**:** a type of fish	We went bass fishing last week.
bass [sounds like *base*]**:** a deep sound or tone	The musician played a bass guitar.

Term/Definition	Example
beat: a verb meaning "to hit or to defeat"	The Yankees beat the Mets in the playoffs.
beet: a vegetable similar to a carrot	We had beets with our dinner.
beside: a preposition meaning "by the side of" or "next to" something	I sat beside her at the table.
besides: a preposition meaning "in addition to" something	Besides being smart, she is pretty.
billed: having been given an invoice for payment; something that has a bill, which is the jaws of a bird or turtle	I was billed for the purchase.
build: a verb meaning to construct	I want to build a model airplane.
blew: the past tense of *blow*	I blew out the candles on the cake.
blue: a color. It also means feeling sad or low in spirit.	When I feel blue I wear my blue sweater.
board: a piece of wood, or a group that runs an organization	We put a board over the broken window.
bored: feeling weary of something, or having drilled a hole	I never get bored when I do my homework.
bow [sounds like *cow*]**:** a verb meaning to bend as a sign of respect	At the end of the concert, the musician bowed.
bow [sounds like *cow*]**:** a noun meaning the front of a ship	The captain stood on the bow and looked toward land.
bow [sounds like *show*]**:** a noun meaning a knot with loops	I tied a bow around the gift.
bow [sounds like *show*]**:** a noun meaning a long, flat piece of wood with strings stretched across it, used for playing musical instruments	The violinist picked up her bow and began to play.
brake: a device used to slow or stop something	The brake on my bicycle is squeaky.
break: a verb meaning "to rest" or "to destroy"	I took a break from writing because I wanted to break open my piggy bank.
buy: a verb meaning "to purchase"	I love to buy clothes.

Term/Definition	Example
by: a preposition meaning "near" or "through"	I live by the sea.
bye: the short form of good-bye. It also means the position of being advanced automatically to the next round of a tournament.	She said "Bye!" when she left.
can: able to	I can run a mile.
may: permitted to	I may have dessert if I eat my dinner.
capital: the head of a state or country; it also means "money"	There are a great deal of people with capital in big cities, like the capital of the state.
capitol: a government building	The capitol is in the center of the city.
cell: a small room or a small unit of life in plants and animals	The religious leader lives in a cell.
sell: a verb meaning "to give away for a price"	I want to sell my car.
cent: a coin	The candy costs five cents.
scent: a smell	The flowers have a strong scent.
sent: the past tense of the verb *send*	I sent the package to her yesterday.
chord: three or more musical notes being played at the same time; it can also mean a feeling	The chords in the song struck a chord with me.
cord: a string	We tied the newspapers up with cord.
cite: a verb meaning "to quote"	I cited my sources for the research paper.
sight: the act of seeing or a thing that is seen.	It was love at first sight.
site: a place or location	The site of the festival was a large field.
close [sounds like *nose*]**:** a verb meaning to shut something	Please close the door when you leave.
close [sounds like *nose*]**:** a verb meaning to end something	Close your essay with a strong conclusion paragraph
close [sounds like *gross*]**:** an adverb meaning near	Stay close to me when we're in a crowded place.
close [sounds like *gross*]**:** an adjective meaning care-ful	Keep a close eye on the dog when he's in the yard.

Term/Definition	Example
close [sounds like *gross*]**:** an adjective meaning almost even	The score of the baseball game was close.
coarse: rough	My father's beard is coarse.
course: a path or direction; it also means a class in school	I choose to follow a different course by taking math courses.
complement: a verb meaning "to complete" or "to fit well with"	That scarf complements her outfit.
compliment: an expression of praise	The compliment made me feel happy.
could have: a verbal phrase not to be misspelled as "could of" (which never, never makes sense!) **would have:** a verbal phrase not to be misspelled as "would of" (again, never write this!)	I could have gone swimming, but I would have needed to put on my bathing suit.
council: a group that advises	The council determined that she should be in charge.
counsel: a noun meaning "advice", or a verb meaning "to advise"	My teacher gave me counsel about how to do the assignment.
creak: a squeaking sound	The door creaked when I opened it.
creek: a stream	I dipped my toes in the creek.
cymbal: a musical instrument	The drummer hit the cymbal.
symbol: something that stands for or represents something else	Hearts are a symbol of love.
dear: an adjective meaning "loved" or "valued"	My friend is dear to me.
deer: a type of animal	The deer ran into the forest.
desert [sounds like *dez*-ert]: a noun meaning "a barren area"	The camel roamed the desert.
desert [sounds like dez-*ert*]: a verb meaning "to leave or withdraw"	The guide deserted us in the middle of the woods!
dessert [sounds like dez-*ert*]: a treat at the end of a meal	I had ice cream for dessert.

Term/Definition	Example
die: a verb meaning "to stop living"	He died of old age.
dye: a verb meaning "to change the color" of something; also a noun meaning the substance used to change the color of something	I used dye to dye the shirt.
emigrate: to leave one's own country to go live in another	I am going to emigrate from Canada.
immigrate: to come into a new country to live permanently	She immigrated here years ago.
farther: an adverb used with physical distance	She ran farther than he was able to.
further: an adverb or adjective meaning "more or additional"	I need to give further information.
fir: a type of evergreen tree	We decorated a fir tree.
fur: animal hair	The dog's fur is all over the couch.
flair: an ability or talent	She has a flair for the dramatic.
flare: a verb meaning "to light up quickly"	The fire flared when he added more wood.
for: a preposition meaning "because of" or "instructed to"	She was sad, for her grandmother was sick.
fore-: a prefix meaning "earlier" or "at the front"	She was at the forefront of the movement.
four: a number	I am four years old.
goes: a variation of the verb *go*, meaning "to proceed" or "to move"	She often goes to the park.
says: a variation of *say*, meaning "to express or speak"; *goes* should never be used in place of *says*	She says that I am a good student.
good: most often an adjective to describe a noun	We had a good time at the party.
well: most often an adverb to describe an action	I performed well at the concert.
hair: the growth covering the bodies of mammals	My dad is losing his hair!
hare: an animal similar to a rabbit	The hare jumped into the bushes.
hanged: suspended by the neck until dead	The villain was hanged.

Term/Definition	Example
hung: suspended	I hung the plant from the ceiling.
heal: a verb meaning "to mend"	The medicine will help the cut heal.
heel: the back part of a foot	The shoes make my heels hurt.
hear: a verb meaning "to perceive by using the ear"	I can hear the birds chirping.
here: a set location or place	He lives here.
heard: the past tense of the verb *hear*, meaning "to perceive by using the ear"	I heard the bells of the church this morning.
herd: a group of animals	The shepherd gathered his herd.
heir: a person who inherits something	He is the heir to the throne.
air: the mixture of gases that surround the Earth	The air is cool this evening.
hole: a cavity	There is a hole in my sweater!
whole: an adjective meaning "entire" or "complete"	The dog ate the whole cake.
imply: to indirectly suggest something	She implied that she knew the secret.
infer: to draw a conclusion based on facts	Based on the data, we can infer that it is a good decision.
in: a preposition meaning "inside something"	The cake is in the oven.
into: a verb meaning "to move toward the inside of something from another place"	I'm putting the cake into the oven.
it's: the contraction used to say *it is*	It's fun to dance!
its: the possessive form of the word *it*	The dog chased its tail.
knew: past tense of the verb *know*, meaning "to be aware of" or "to understand"	I knew the answer to the question.
new: an adjective meaning "recent" or "modern"	I bought new clothes for school.
know: a verb meaning "to be aware of" or "to understand"	I know I can make the team.
no: a negative response	She said no when I asked her for permission.
lay: a verb meaning "to put something somewhere"	I will lay the book on the desk.

Term/Definition	Example
lie: a verb meaning "to make a false statement" or "to rest or recline"	I need to lie down.
lead [sounds like *weed*]**:** a verb meaning "to guide"	I have to lead the horse around the ring.
lead [sounds like *weed*]**:** a verb meaning "to be in charge"	The teacher leads the class discussion.
lead [sounds like *weed*]**:** a noun meaning "the front position"	The brown horse took the lead in the race.
lead [sounds like *weed*]**:** a noun meaning "a helpful piece of information"	The detective found a new lead in the case.
lead [sounds like *weed*]**:** a noun meaning "the main role in a play or movie"	I earned the lead in my school play.
lead [sounds like *weed*]**:** a noun meaning "a leash"	I attached the dog to his lead.
lead [sounds like *red*]**:** a noun that means "a type of metal"	The old pipes were made of lead.
led [sounds like *red*]**:** past tense of the verb *lead,* which means "to guide"	I led the horse around the ring.
learn: to obtain and understand information	I had to learn the multiplication tables.
teach: to give information	My mom wanted to teach me to cook.
like: a preposition meaning "similar to" something; also a verb meaning "to enjoy or to feel inclined toward" something	I like outfits that make me look like a movie star.
as: a conjunction meaning "while" or "to the same degree"	She is as free as a bird.
made: past tense of the verb *make*, meaning "to create"	I made cookies!
maid: a service person. It also means "a young girl."	The maid came in to clean the hotel room.
mail: letters or packages sent through the postal service	I took the mail out of the box.
male: the masculine gender	The new baby is male, not female.

Term/Definition	Example
main: the most important part	The main idea of the story is that people should be kind.
mane: hair growing from the neck of an animal	The horse's mane was braided.
meat: the flesh of an animal	We had meat, potatoes, and carrots for dinner.
meet: a verb meaning "to encounter"	I want to meet the new student.
medal: an award	The athlete won a medal.
meddle: a verb meaning "to interfere in" something	My mom often meddles in my life.
metal: an element	The pot is made of metal.
mettle: strength of spirit	The soldier showed mettle in battle.
miner: one who digs for valuable things in the ground	The coal miner's face was dusty.
minor: an adjective meaning "of less importance"; also a person who is not an adult	She is still a minor, so the offense is minor.
morning: the earliest part of a day	I have to wake up for school in the morning.
mourning: a verb meaning "to feel and express sadness"	After her dad died, she was mourning.
oar: a paddle used to row a boat	I used an oar to move the rowboat.
or: a conjunction that indicates choice	You can have one or the other.
ore: a mineral	The miner found ore in the canyon.
pain: a bad feeling	I felt pain when I broke my arm.
pane: a section of something	The pane of the window was broken.
pair: two of something	I bought a pair of socks.
pare: a verb meaning "to reduce or peel"	I pared the skin of the apple.
pear: a fruit	Pears are juicy.
passed: a verb meaning "to go or proceed"	She passed me in the hall.
past: a preposition meaning "move by"; a noun meaning "a time before the present"	In the past, I walked past the house.

Term/Definition	Example
peace: harmony	There is seldom peace between the two kids.
piece: a part of a whole	I ate a piece of the apple.
plain: a flat area of land; not interesting in appearance; clearly seen or understood	It was plain to see that the girl was plain.
plane: a level surface	A football field is a plane.
poor: an adjective meaning "in need"	The poor victims of the tragedy need help.
pore: an opening in the skin	My pore had dirt in it, so I got a pimple.
pour: a verb meaning "to make a constant flow"	Pour a glass of milk for me.
present [sounds like *resent*]**:** a verb meaning "to give a gift or prize in a formal way"	I have to present the winner with a trophy.
present [sounds like *resent*]**:** a verb meaning "to introduce"	The anchorperson presents the news.
present [sounds like *pleasant*]**:** a noun meaning "something that you give someone"	I gave the birthday girl a present.
present [sounds like *pleasant*]**:** a noun meaning "the current time"	There is no time like the present.
present [sounds like *pleasant*]**:** an adjective meaning that a person or thing is here	I said that I was present during attendance.
principal: an adjective meaning "primary"; also a noun referring to a school administrator or a sum of money	I was called to the principal's office.
principle: an idea or belief	America was founded on the principle of freedom.
produce [sounds like *reduce*]**:** a verb meaning "to make something"	Carpenters produce furniture.
produce [sounds like *reduce*]**:** a verb meaning "to bring something out for others to see"	I produced the coin from my pocket.
produce [sounds like *reduce*]**:** a verb meaning "to be in charge of making a movie, TV show, or play"	He produced a great movie.

Term/Definition	Example
produce [sounds like *proe-dewss*]: a noun meaning "things that are grown to be eaten," like fruit and vegetables	Apples and oranges are my favorite produce.
raise: a verb meaning "to elevate"	We raise our hands when we want to speak.
rays: thin lines or beams	The sun has many rays.
raze: a verb meaning "to completely tear down"	The old theater was razed to make room for a new one.
read: a verb meaning "to understand the meaning of words"	I read the directions carefully.
red: a color	I am wearing a red shirt.
right: an adjective meaning "correct." It also means the direction opposite of left, or anything that some-one has a legal claim to.	I gave the right answer to the question.
rite: a ritual	Summer camp is a rite of passage for kids.
write: to record something in print	I have to write a poem.
scene: a location where something happens, or a spectacle	The police arrived at the scene of the crime.
seen: past tense of the verb *see*, meaning "to view"	I have already seen this movie.
seam: the place where two pieces of material meet when they are sewn together	My shirt ripped at the seam.
seem: a verb meaning "to appear to be" a certain way	Your mother seems well.
sew: a verb meaning "to stitch"	I have to sew a button on my shirt.
so: a conjunction meaning "in order that"	I left school early so I could go to the doctor.
sow: a verb meaning "to plant"	We sowed the field.
sit: to place a body in a seated position.	I told the dog to sit.
set: to place	I set the napkin on the table.
soar: a verb meaning "to fly high above"	The birds soar above us.

Term/Definition	Example
sore: an adjective meaning "painfully sensitive", or an open wound	After practice, my muscles are sore.
sole: an adjective meaning "only one"; also a noun meaning "the bottom of a foot or shoe" or a type of fish	There is a hole in the sole of my shoe.
soul: a noun that means "the spiritual part of a person"	She has a kind soul.
some: an unknown number of things, or part	Some of us will go to the party.
sum: a total amount	The sum of two and two is four.
stationary: an adjective meaning "in a fixed place, not movable"	I rode the stationary bike for exercise.
stationery: paper used to write notes or letters	I wrote a letter to my grandmother on flowered stationery.
steal: to take something without permission	The runner decided to steal second base.
steel: a metal	The pot is made from stainless steel.
tear [sounds like *here*]**:** a noun meaning "a drop of clear liquid produced by the eye"	A tear ran down her cheek.
tear [sounds like *there*]**:** a noun meaning "a rip"	There is a tear in my paper.
tear [sounds like *there*]**:** a verb meaning "to be pulled apart"	Tear up the old shirt to use as rags.
their: a plural possessive pronoun that shows ownership	The boys love their new coats.
there: an adverb specifying the idea of where	If I run, I will get there first.
they're: the contraction meaning "they are"	They're going to the dance together.
threw: the past tense of the verb *throw*, meaning "to propel" something	Amy threw the ball to me.
through: a preposition meaning "passing from one side to another"	It crashed through the window.
to: a preposition meaning "in the direction of"	I am going to the baseball game.

Term/Definition	Example
too: adverb meaning "very" or "also"	I put one too many eggs in the recipe.
two: a number	There are two socks in a pair.
vain: an adjective meaning "thinking highly of yourself"	She is vain because she thinks she is the prettiest one.
vane: a tool that shows which direction the wind blows	The weather vane pointed south.
vein: a blood vessel	When my mother gets mad, the vein in her forehead pops out.
waist: the part of the body above the hips	That woman has a tiny waist.
waste: a verb meaning "to wear away"; also a noun meaning "unused"	I made so much food that some of it went to waste.
wait: to stay	She told me to sit patiently and wait.
wait for: to stay until something happens	I have to wait for her to pick me up from school.
wait on: to serve someone	I wait on the patrons of the diner.
weight: the measure of heaviness	When I stood on the scale, I saw that I had lost weight.
ware: a product for sale	The peddler sold his wares.
wear: a verb meaning "to have on one's body"	I have nothing to wear to the party!
where: a place or situation	I don't know where I left my backpack.
way: a noun meaning "route"	I know the way to the stream.
weigh: a verb meaning "to measure weight"	The doctor weighed the newborn baby.
weak: an adjective meaning "not strong"	I felt weak when I had the chicken pox.
week: seven days	I have a doctor's appointment next week.
weather: the condition of the atmosphere	The weather has been pleasant recently.
whether: a possibility	I have to see whether I am allowed to go or not.
which: a pronoun that points something out	I don't know the direction in which to walk.
witch: a person with supernatural powers	I dressed as a witch for Halloween.

Term/Definition	Example
who: a pronoun used to refer to people	My sister is a girl who enjoys playing with dolls.
which: refers to nonliving things and sometimes animals or creatures, but never to people	I have a fear of heights, which makes it difficult to climb mountains.
that: can refer to people, animals, or things	I have a cat that loves whipped cream.
who: use as the subject in a sentence	Who is making all that noise?
whom: use as the object of a preposition, or a direct object	I have a secret and I don't know whom to tell!
who's: a contraction meaning "who is"	Who's at the door?
whose: a possessive pronoun that shows ownership	Whose dog is running loose?
wind [sounds like *grinned*]**:** a noun meaning "air that is moving"	The wind blew the branches of the tree.
wind [sounds like *grinned*]**:** a noun meaning "breath"	The ball hit me in the belly and knocked the wind out of me.
wind [sounds like *kind*]**:** a verb meaning "to wrap something around"	Wind the lights around the Christmas tree.
wind [sounds like *kind*]**:** a verb meaning "to twist"	The road winds down the mountain.
wood: material that trees are made of	We used wood to build the tree house.
would: a form of *will*, meaning "consent" or "probability"	I would like to go to the beach.
your: a possessive pronoun that shows ownership	I like your new car.
you're: a contraction meaning "you are"	You're a good friend.